MW00714117

# CHICAGO CUBS COOKBOOK
## All-Star Recipes from Your Favorite Players

Edited by Carrie Muskat

Copyright © 2010 Chicago Cubs

No part of this publication may be reproduced, stored in a retrieval system, or transmitted in any form by any means, electronic, mechanical, photocopying, or otherwise, without the prior written permission of the publisher, Triumph Books, 542 South Dearborn Street, Suite 750, Chicago, Illinois 60605.

Triumph Books and colophon are registered trademarks of Random House, Inc.

This book is available in quantity at special discounts for your group or organization. For further information, contact:

**Triumph Books**
542 South Dearborn Street
Suite 750
Chicago, Illinois 60605
(312) 939-3330
Fax (312) 663-3557
www.triumphbooks.com

Printed in U.S.A.
ISBN: 978-1-60078-527-6
Design and page production by Wagner Donovan Design
Photos courtesy of Stephen Green Photography and Bob Milkovich Photography & Marketing

# Contents

## Lineup of Recipes

### Leading Off: Appetizers

### Pinch Hitters: Side Dishes

## Heart of the Order: Main Courses

# Foreword

There is talk in baseball and other professional sports about "courageous performances." The term is overused and somewhat of a cliché—unless you are talking about four remarkable individuals who will always be members of the Chicago Cubs family: Ryan, Jenny, Brady, and Riley Dempster.

Riley Dempster is one of the most beautiful fans in Cubs nation. She is not yet 2 years old, but she has already exhibited the real definition of courage. She is active and energetic—her parents are always chasing after her, whether she is following big brother, Brady, or splashing in the dog's water bowl. Riley doesn't let anything get her down; not even the feeding tube she uses to take in calories because, since birth, she has suffered a rare and still-mysterious disorder called DiGeorge syndrome. Children stricken by DiGeorge syndrome, or 22q, suffer from a variety of health problems including heart defects, cleft palates, immune deficiency, and, in some cases, a spectrum of developmental issues. DiGeorge is caused by deletions of genetic material in the 22q11.2 chromosome.

Riley's determination to catch her brother or torment the family dogs is an inspiration. In that way, she takes after her parents, Ryan and Jenny, and brother, Brady. It never occurred to Jenny to withdraw into herself once her baby was diagnosed with 22q. Jenny and Ryan and the Dempster family advocate for Riley every day and still have time and energy to do the same for all of the children suffering from this disorder. Lifelong volunteers who have always given of their time, talent, and treasure to raise money for charity, Jenny and Ryan formed the Dempster

Family Foundation to raise money for medical research, education, and support services for parents of DiGeorge children and for physical therapy for the children.

Ryan Dempster, with his fierce competitiveness and the focus, discipline, and self-sacrifice he brings to the pitching mound, is one of the gutsiest performers on the Cubs. But he's only the fourth most courageous member of his young family compared to Riley, Jenny, and young Brady. Ryan dedicates himself every game to leaving everything he has on the field. But his real passion is making a difference in the lives of these children, and especially for one little girl named Riley, whose father melts whenever she is in his arms.

On behalf of my brothers, Pete and Todd, and our sister, Laura, we are delighted to be a part of this cookbook to help support the cause of the Dempster Family Foundation. Of the dishes featured in the book, I confess to having eaten only the Ricketts family sugar cookies. Our mom found the original recipe, and we humbly include it in this cookbook and look forward to sharing our family tradition with yours for a cause greater than our own.

**Tom Ricketts**
**Chairman, Chicago Cubs**

# Publisher's Note

Carrie Muskat was the visionary and driving force behind this project. Back in spring training, Carrie began soliciting players to participate as a way to give back to their friend and teammate Ryan Dempster. Carrie contacted people throughout the extended Cubs organization—players, managers, coaches, broadcasters, alums, even the Ricketts family—and found a way for everyone to participate whether they had a favorite recipe to share or not. She did all this—and facilitated a couple of photo shoots—under great time pressure, while working and traveling for her very demanding "day job" as the lead Cubs writer for MLB.com. Without Carrie's impassioned hustle and focus, this book would never have been developed or completed.

Bob Milkovich of Milkovich Photography & Marketing stepped up to the plate in a big way to pull together a couple of unconventional player photo shoots that gave real life to the cookbook.

Special thanks to Eileen Wagner of Wagner Donovan Design for juggling all the disparate pieces on her way to designing a wonderful book and to John Morrison of the Cubs, who made sure all eyes remained focused on the ultimate goal—producing a great product that fans will want to call their own, enabling much money to be raised for the Dempster Family Foundation. Cubs Executive Vice President and Chief Sales and Marketing Officer Wally Hayward made the project a real priority, encouraging other talented and enthusiastic folks like Anna Rivera and Joe Rios to contribute their time and energy. Thanks to Ann Pendleton of Levy Restaurants for taking such an active role and to a pal, Steve Green of Stephen Green Photography, for making his awesome Cubs photo archive available to us.

This project reminds me of how lucky I am to have an incredibly talented and committed team to work with here at Triumph. The cookbook team was led off by production manager Kris Anstrats and managing editor Don Gulbrandsen, along with Karen O'Brien and Paul Petrowsky. Natalie King, Fred Walski, Phil Springstead, and Mindi Rowland from the marketing and promotion side soon joined the effort. Bill Swanson, our ever-present operations manager, kept all the moving parts from colliding. Collectively, the team did whatever was necessary to produce a book everyone involved could be proud of.

Most importantly, thanks to Ryan and Jenny Dempster for all they are doing to help and comfort others.

**Mitch Rogatz**
**President, Triumph Books**

# Introduction

It was right after the 2008 season. Cubs pitcher Ted Lilly and the team's bullpen catcher, Corey Miller, were having lunch at a California sushi restaurant, and the conversation switched to fundraising.

A catcher on another team was doing some work on a community project, Corey said. Why couldn't the Cubs do something as a team? And between bites of raw fish, they agreed on this: Wouldn't it be cool if Cubs players could help somebody by creating a cookbook with their own recipes?

Fast-forward to February 2010, Mesa, Arizona, spring training. Corey approached me with the idea and about my being part of the project. I laughed. Aside from attempts at making by grandmother's noodle pudding for family events (sometimes I get it right, sometimes not), I don't cook. My husband likes to cook. I clean up after his mess.

As the Cubs beat writer for MLB.com, for much of the year I eat the majority of my meals in major league ballparks or off trays in hotel rooms. When I'm home and my husband isn't stirring up something, well, Chicago has some of the best restaurants in the world. Most of them deliver.

But when Ted and Corey said they wanted proceeds from the cookbook sale to go to Ryan Dempster's foundation, I was in.

Ryan's daughter, Riley, is battling 22q11.2 deletion (DiGeorge syndrome/VCFS), a disorder caused by a deletion on the 22q11.2 chromosome. To put it in English: the disorder impedes her ability to feed and swallow.

"I wouldn't wish this on my worst enemy," Ryan said.

Through the foundation, Ryan and his wife, Jenny, are trying to make life easier not just for Riley but for others with 22q. "The story isn't 'Ryan Dempster's kid,'" he says. "It's kids in general."

Cubs players past, present, and future, plus coaches and others involved with the game were asked for recipes. The result is an eclectic mix, from Carlos Silva's arepas to Marlon Byrd's ziti. When we asked restaurants to reveal some of their secrets—for Ryan Dempster and his foundation—the answer was always an enthusiastic "Yes." Their recipes are in the book as well.

This is my second book. I had two years to work on the first, *Banks to Sandberg to Grace* (Contemporary Books, 2001). We had months to work on this one, and it could not have been done without a great team.

Thanks to Shelley Jaramillo for her suggestions and support, and to all the Cubs wives and significant others who sent emails or filled out index cards with recipes—and then helped this non-cook decipher them. Thanks to the Chicago restaurants who shared their specialties. Thanks to my husband, Alan, and sister, Jeanne, for testing these. We've been eating pretty well.

Thanks to the folks at Triumph Books, including Mitch Rogatz and Don Gulbrandsen, and to designer Eileen Wagner. Photographer Bob Milkovich created some unique shots of the Cubs players you won't see anywhere else. It was a Herculean effort by all.

Thanks to Otis Hellman, Gary Stark, Tim Hellman, and Rich Rupp for letting me use their clubhouse space. Thanks to Ed Hartig for researching food-related Cubs tidbits. Thanks to Terri Grunduski for her support.

Thanks to Tom Ricketts for the go-ahead and to Laura Ricketts for sharing the family cookie recipe. And, many thanks to the Cubs—Wally Hayward, John Morrison, Joe Rios, Peter Chase, Jason Carr, Dani Holmes, Jim Hendry, Anna Rivera, Vijay Tekchandani, Stephen Green, and Mary Dosek—who believed in this and helped make it happen for Ryan Dempster and his little girl.

"Demp" is special, to his family and to his teammates. He can do impersonations of Harry Caray, and he can do magic tricks. Someday he might appear on stage at a comedy club near you. He's been known to wear outrageous outfits in the clubhouse. And he's special to the women and men who cover the Chicago Cubs. When things get tough in the clubhouse—and that's been known to happen—he's there for us.

When it comes to his job as pitcher for the Cubs, Ryan is one of the toughest competitors in the game. Riley has inherited that spirit. She still has a tough fight ahead of her.

This is for the Dempsters. And this is for kids in general.

**Carrie Muskat**

# The Ryan and Jenny Dempster Family Foundation

On her first birthday in April 2010, Riley Dempster made a mess of her birthday cake. It was a beautiful thing. She was covered in frosting and—best of all—she could even taste it. Think about how easy it is to swallow your drink. You probably don't even think about it. You take a swig and done.

It's not the same for Riley. She has 22q11.2 deletion, or DiGeorge syndrome/VCFS, which is a common, yet largely unknown disorder caused by a deletion in the 22nd chromosome. Symptoms vary with different degrees of severity. In Riley's case, her biggest obstacle is feeding and swallowing. Her esophagus lacks the motility to swallow even the natural secretions that her body produces. Riley has been through numerous surgeries and procedures in her young life: from a tracheostomy to keep her lungs clear of the fluids she cannot swallow, to a Nissen Fundoplication to reduce reflux, to placement of a G-tube for feeding her directly into her belly.

She's survived it all. Riley is one tough little lady.

"I think what a strong woman it's going to make her," Ryan said of his daughter. "Nobody's going to be able to tell her she can't do something. If she can get through all this, she can get through everything."

Riley has a strong team backing her, including dad Ryan, mom Jenny, and brother Brady. "When we first received Riley's diagnosis, we researched everything we could find," Jenny said. "We spent countless hours scouring the Internet and calling every doctor we knew. We were amazed and frustrated at the lack of information out there, especially considering that 22q is the second most common chromosomal disorder next to Down syndrome.

"There were so many things that the specialists told us Riley would not do on time, if at all," Jenny said. "At one point we were even told that Riley couldn't swallow, and may have her feeding tube and trach her entire life. Ryan and I decided that Riley *didn't* swallow, rather then *couldn't* swallow, and she's proved us right. On her first birthday, in front of her friends and family, Riley swallowed the icing from her birthday cake. We all watched anxiously for any sign of the icing to come out of her trach, but there was none! It was a momentous occasion!"

Riley still requires 24-hour nursing care and weekly sessions with physical therapists and speech therapists and monthly sessions with occupational and developmental therapists. But with the hard work of everyone involved, Riley is hitting developmental milestones on target. She has even learned to block her trach to make noise when she wants to, and is speaking with the help of a Passy-Muir valve.

There's still a long way to go, but because of the early diagnoses and care, she's on her way. "The key to Riley's success undoubtedly has been the early diagnosis," Jenny said. "We were able to know what we were dealing with and get her the care she needed from the very beginning. It has made all the difference in where Riley is today, and is why we are so passionate about educating people about this syndrome. So many children and adults go years without a diagnosis, because not all people are affected in the same way, or with the same severity. Any one of us may know someone with the deletion, maybe your own child, or a niece or nephew, or a child of a friend. Knowing the signs and symptoms is so important."

In an effort to raise awareness and help the cause, the Cubs players created this cookbook, with the proceeds to benefit the Ryan and Jenny Dempster Family Foundation.

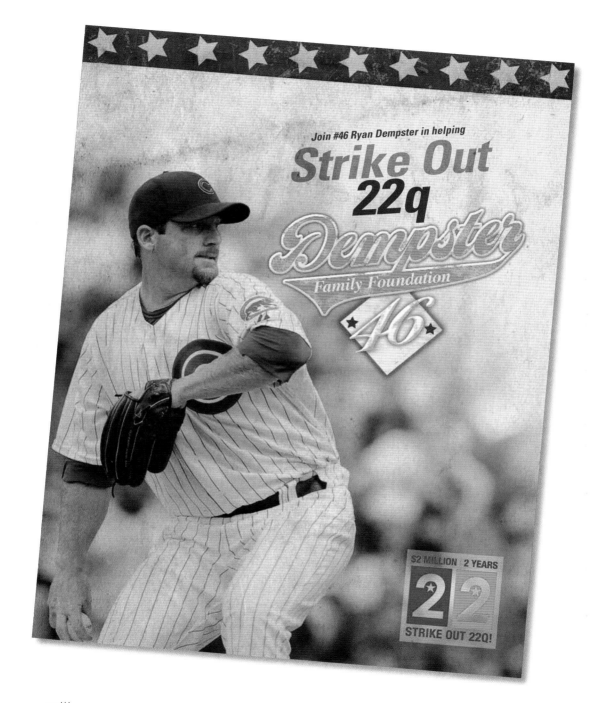

Join #46 Ryan Dempster in helping

# Strike Out
## 22q

Dempster
Family Foundation
46

$2 MILLION | 2 YEARS
22
STRIKE OUT 22Q!

# Ryan and Jenny Dempster Family Foundation

## Vision Statement

The Ryan and Jenny Dempster Family Foundation is dedicated to raising awareness of 22q11.2 deletion (DiGeorge syndrome/Velo-cardiofacial syndrome or VCFS) and reaching out to families with children with the disorder, and the charities that support them, to help them deal with the challenges they face every day.

## Mission Statement

The Ryan and Jenny Dempster Family Foundation lends support to charities and other organizations helping children with 22q11.2 deletion (DiGeorge syndrome/VCFS) through monetary grants, educational and fundraising programs, and increased community awareness. The Dempster Foundation empowers organizations to help children with rare illnesses overcome difficult situations through:

- providing funding to continue research for early detection of this disorder in children
- supporting programs about 22q that provide education, physical therapy, and activity to promote long-term well-being
- creating initiatives that build and instill confidence in these children
- developing a 22q network for families affected by this disorder to share stories and help navigate heathcare options and treatment

For more information on the foundation, please visit the website at: dempsterfamilyfoundation.org.

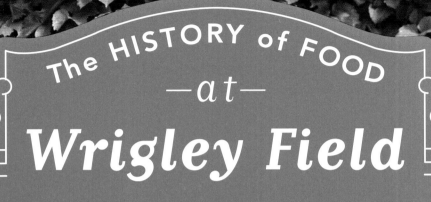

# The HISTORY of FOOD
# —at—
# Wrigley Field

**The following history** and timeline of Wrigley foodstuff was provided by Cubs historian Ed Hartig. In the 1930s, fans could buy 12 different food items at Wrigley Field, from a bottle of near beer to 10-cent red hots (hot dogs). Buy a ticket to a Cubs game now, and you better come hungry. The menu has expanded to 54 food products, from Big Slugger nachos, which stuffs 2 lbs. of sour cream, black olives, chili, nacho cheese, hot peppers, and chips into a mini batting helmet, to a High Plains Bison burger. On an average weekend in 2010, Cubs fans consume 36,000 hot dogs and wash them down with 62,000 glasses of draft beer. Even the players have upgraded their game-day eating. There's now a six-burner stainless steel stove so clubhouse manager Tom "Otis" Hellman can feed 25 players, six coaches, one manager, and the athletic training staff. In the old days, players would send one of the clubhouse kids out to the concourse to buy food.

*1914:* Hoping to make it easier for patrons to purchase food, the Chicago Federals introduced a vending system using a long rod and basket to pass items to fans, similar to a church collection basket. The purchaser would place money in the basket, the vendor would pull in the basket, and then pass the food back to the fan. However, it didn't work too well. Owner Charlie Weeghman came up with the idea of setting up kiosks in the rear of the grandstand where customers could buy food and then return to their seats. This evolved to the first permanent concession stands in all of baseball.

**1930s:** Vendors at Wrigley Field were easy to spot based on the color of their cap. Fans wanting peanuts looked for vendors wearing a brown cap, while those hoping for popcorn watched out for blue caps. Other vendor cap colors included: red for red hots (aka hot dogs); yellow for lemonade; white for ice cream; green for soda pop; gray for scorecards; wine-colored for candy and gum; and black for cigarettes.

 *1932:* The Cubs reached the World Series this year, only to lose to the Yankees in four games. Fans could buy a bottle of Near Beer for 20 cents, gum for 5 cents, a cup of coffee or a red hot for 10 cents each, and a glass of lemonade for 15 cents.

**March 1933:** Despite the end of prohibition, the debate about whether or not to sell beer at games divided team owners. Both the Cubs and White Sox decided to sell beer at their games but followed a league-wide policy that beer would not be dispensed in the stands.

 *January 10, 1934:* William Walker, the Cubs' new president following the October death of Bill Veeck Sr., announced the team would continue its ban on selling hard liquor at the park. However, Walker did say beer sale efforts would be expanded. In 1933 the Cubs only were able to sell bottled beer at the bars under the stands. In 1934 the plan was to dispense beer both in bottles and from taps, and beer in containers would be available in the stands.

*1936:* If the peanuts sold at Wrigley Field during the '36 season were laid end to end, they would reach from the ballpark to Aurora, Illinois. If the pop bottles were stacked end to end in a one-foot square, they would form a tower more than twice as high as the Empire State Building. Also, enough red hots were sold in a season to provide two each to every resident in the towns of Aurora, Evanston, Wilmette, and Kenilworth, Illinois—along with a cup of coffee. Three tons of sugar was used in 1935 for coffee and lemonade. The team popped five tons of popcorn. The Cubs also used nearly 1 million paper cups.

 *July 4-5, 1937:* The concession department sold 60,000 red hots for the double-headers versus Pittsburgh and St. Louis. That's three tons of hot dogs. They also went through 11,000 ham, cheese, and hot roast beef sandwiches; 19,200 candy bars; 16,000 bags of peanuts; 11,280 bags of popcorn; 600 loaves of bread; 18,000 packages of ice cream; 19,200 cans of beer; 18 barrels of beer; 6,000 lemonades; and 41,000 bottles of pop.

 *1938:* Wrigley Field's concessions department underwent a major $30,000 renovation. New tile-and-brick dispensaries were erected along with storerooms housing the latest in food service equipment. State-of-the art hot dog cookers, popcorn poppers, and peanut warmers were added.

 *1938:* More than 1,500 vendors were employed during the season. On days with a small crowd, about 75 vendors were on the job. For large crowds, the numbers increased from 200 to 250. The vendors generated about 80 percent of the park's concession business from 17 items.

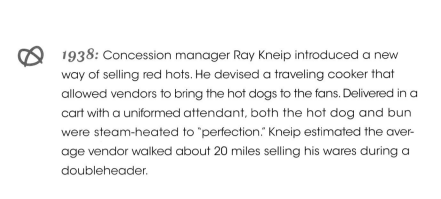 **1938:** Concession manager Ray Kneip introduced a new way of selling red hots. He devised a traveling cooker that allowed vendors to bring the hot dogs to the fans. Delivered in a cart with a uniformed attendant, both the hot dog and bun were steam-heated to "perfection." Kneip estimated the average vendor walked about 20 miles selling his wares during a doubleheader.

**1938:** The Cubs win the National League pennant but lose again to the Yankees in four games in the World Series. A glass of lemonade or can of beer at the ballpark was 20 cents each and a red hot was 10 cents.

**1941:** Ray Kneip, head of concessions since 1927, announced many new menu choices for Wrigley including a new variety of jumbo peanuts grown in Virginia. They also added new popcorn never before sold in ballparks that was made from South American corn grown in Iowa. It was given a boost with the addition of butter and salt. Fans now could purchase juicy, all-beefsteak hamburgers spiced with salt, pepper, onions, or piccalilli. Still a favorite: Oscar Meyer yellow-band frankfurters with mustard and relish and well-buttered roast beef or baked ham sandwiches.

**1941:** Concessions manager Ray Kneip estimated Cubs fans ate 298,450 hot dogs and 94,680 hamburgers at Wrigley during the season.

**July 1942:** In one week of the Cubs homestand from July 9–19, Wrigley vendors sold more than 15,000 cups of "Pure Lemo" lemonade. On July 12, they went through 13 tons of ice to keep the lemonade cool.

*1943:* Unable to get high-grade beef because of wartime shortages, the Cubs stopped selling hamburgers at Wrigley. The hot dogs also were affected as Oscar Meyer switched to a red hot that was skinless, shorter, plumper, and heavier than previous years.

 *June 27, 1943:* It was a record-setting day concession-wise at Wrigley as 37,712 fans sat through rain delays to watch the Cubs and Cardinals in a Sunday doubleheader. They consumed 35,600 hot dogs; 5,550 bags of peanuts; 3,020 bags of popcorn; 30,200 bottles of soda pop; 5,240 glasses of lemonade; 25,700 cups of ice cream; 32,000 bottles of beer; 11,724 scorecards; and 1,000 sets of team photographs. The concessionaires needed 11 tons of ice to keep the food chilled. Unfortunately, the Cubs were cold, too, losing both games by scores of 3–2 and 4–3.

*June 24, 1945:* With a crowd of more than 42,000 attending the Cubs-Cardinals doubleheader, the concession stands set records to top the '43 marks. The staff of 250 sold 72,000 red hots; 5,000 baked ham sandwiches; 5,000 roast beef sandwiches; 22,000 bottles of pop; 30,000 beers; 24,000 bags of peanuts; and 17,000 bags of popcorn. The Cubs split the twinbill, losing the first game, 8–2 and winning the second, 6–3.

 *1945:* The most recent year the Cubs reached the World Series, you could buy a bottle of beer at Wrigley Field for 25 cents. Red hots were 15 cents and a glass of lemonade was 20 cents. The vendors were busy as this series went seven games, but the Cubs lost again, this time to the Detroit Tigers, 4–3.

**1946:** Cubs patrons consumed 103,238 lbs. of red hots—totaling 1.24 million hot dogs—during the season. Fans also consumed 864,392 bottles of beer.

 **1949:** In the 1949 season, Kneip said Wrigley customers consumed 1,033,000 red hots; 16,000 lbs. of ham; 3,000 lbs. of cheese; 8,000 loaves of bread; 6,866 lbs. of coffee; 41,000 cases of beer; 43,700 cases of pop; 73,000 lbs. of peanuts; 48,300 dozen ice creams bars; 18,400 lbs. of popcorn. In one doubleheader in '49, the concessions went through 4,000 cases of beer and 23,000 bags of peanuts.

 *June 8, 1950:* Ray Kneip, head of Wrigley Field concessions, told the *Chicago Tribune* in an interview that on a good Sunday doubleheader, a beer vendor can make $45 to $50. Most of the cooking is done prior to the gates opening to minimize loss because of rainouts. He also revealed that automatic poppers in the kitchen can pop 6,000 bags of popcorn in three hours.

**1952:** Typical consumption of 35,000 fans at a Sunday doubleheader game at Wrigley Field was 54,000 red hots; 36,000 bottles of soft drinks; 57,600 bottles of beer; 12,000 bags of popcorn; 12,000 bags of peanuts; 4,000 12-ounce cups of lemonade; 4,000 barbecue sandwiches; 4,000 other sandwiches; and 500 gallons of coffee. The Cubs would use from 100 to 125 vendors plus 80 counter help in six stands around the park.

 **1953:** Ernie Banks made his debut with the Cubs this year on September 17. Beer was 30 cents, red hots were 20 cents, and a BBQ beef sandwich was 35 cents.

**1955:** In the November 16, 1955, issue of *The Sporting News*, Cubs concessions manager Ray Kneip said only the Cubs and Milwaukee Braves operated their own concessions department. The vendors were not paid a salary but earned a commission of 20 cents on every dollar's worth of merchandise sold with a minimum guarantee of $3 per day. A good vendor could earn $50 to $60 per day. The Cubs concession grossed $700,000 annually, including $50,000-$60,000 from football. The Chicago Bears called Wrigley Field home at that time. During an average baseball season, the Cubs sold 120,000 dozen hot dogs; 6,000 lbs. of ham; 4,800 lbs. of barbecue beef; 4,500 lbs. of coffee; 40,000 cases of beer; and 11,000 cases of Coca-Cola. The Cubs discontinued the sale of hamburgers with onions a few years earlier. The problem was that the onions would spill on the ground and attract flies, which was frowned on by the health department.

**May 28, 1961:** A portable smokie link vending wagon caught fire in the right field box seat section during the sixth inning of a Giants-Cubs game at Wrigley. The fittings on a little propane tank developed a leak and the tank caught fire. Wrigley personnel were unable to put out the flames so fire fighters from the Waveland Avenue station were called.

**September 25, 1966:** Ken Holtzman beat the Dodgers' Sandy Koufax 2–1, scoring the game-winner on Jim Lefebvre's error. There were 21,659 at Wrigley that day. By this time, there were 22 food items, including pizza (cheese or sausage), Oscar Mayer hot dogs (30 cents), and Budweiser, which cost 40 cents. You could get a deal on peanuts—two bags for 25 cents (or one for 15 cents).

*1969:* This is a year Ron Santo would like to forget. The Cubs led the Eastern Division by as many as nine games in mid-August and had a half game lead after play September 9. But the Mets rallied—which is one reason Santo hates New York—and won the division. Fans could drown their sorrows in a 45 cent bottle of beer or a 25 cent glass of lemonade at the ballpark. Hot dogs were 50 cents and a slice of cheese pizza was 40 cents.

*1976:* This year was the Cubs' 100th anniversary as a National League team. Fans could toast with a 65 cent bottle of beer. A frosty malt was 40 cents, a glass of lemonade was 25 cents, and a hot dog was now 50 cents.

*1980:* The 1980 season was the last full season of ownership by the Wrigley family. A bottle of beer and a hot dog now cost $1 apiece. Cracker Jack was 50 cents and popcorn was 40 cents.

*1985:* Levy began its expansion at Wrigley Field. The good news is the company brings its trademark Dessert Cart, first introduced in 1982, which offers gourmet treats delivered to the door of skyboxes and suites.

*July 28, 1989:* A Friday afternoon Mets-Cubs game at Wrigley drew 37,554 fans, and they were hungry and thirsty. The crowd consumed 49,658 glasses of beer; 17,086 glasses of soda; 11,370 hot dogs; 5,967 bags of peanuts; 3,725 ice cream products; 2,712 nachos; 1,132 pizza slices; 1,001 bratwurst; 851 Cracker Jack; and 445 cookies.

*1994:* Wrigley Field concessions started a new early bird program where fans could purchase food at a 25 percent discount the first hour the park was open. Alcohol was excluded from the discount.

*2007:* Ballpark Franks became the official hot dog of the Chicago Cubs.

*June 12, 2008:* The Cubs and Braves play a throwback game at Wrigley in honor of WGN-TV's 60th anniversary of Cubs coverage. The two clubs wore 1948-style uniforms, hot dogs sold for $1, and the first two innings of the TV broadcast were in black and white.

*2010:* The Cubs add High Plains Bison as the team's official lean meat and it's available either as bison hot dogs or bison burgers.

# Levy Restaurants

Levy Restaurants took over the Stadium Club operations at Wrigley Field in 1985 and in 2005 became the ballpark's exclusive concessionaire. We've included recipes for three of Levy's specialties here, including a guide on how to make the perfect Chicago hot dog (remember, no ketchup). A new feature at the ballpark starting in 2010 was the Sheffield Grill, which is open to the public and features a menu that changes every home stand. Opening Day 2010 featured a prime rib sandwich and jambalaya.

If you can't get to Wrigley, these recipes provide a little sample of the great food you're missing. And next time you're at the ballpark, make sure to save room for Levy's decadent desserts.

## House-made Black Bean Veggie Burger

At Levy we like to cover all the bases and make sure there are delicious options for everyone.
Serves 2–4

### Ingredients

- 1/4 cup barbecue sauce
- 1 Tbsp. molasses
- 2 cups canned black beans
- 2 cups brown rice, cooked
- 3/4 cup oat bran
- 3 Tbsp. diced onion
- 1 Tbsp. chopped beets
- 2/3 cup panko bread crumbs
- 1 tsp. chili powder
- 1/4 tsp. ground cumin
- 1/4 tsp. ground black pepper
- 1 Tbsp. kosher salt
- 1 Tbsp. diced pickled jalapeños
- 2 egg whites

### Directions

1. Cook brown rice according to the package directions. Cool completely.

2. Drain black beans and mash in a medium-sized bowl. Add the beets, bread crumbs, barbecue sauce, molasses, onions, and jalapeños. Hand-mix thoroughly.

3. Add rice, oats, egg whites, and spices and hand-mix thoroughly. Separate mixture and form into 6 oz. patties.

4. Add 1 tsp. olive oil to a skillet, heat, and add patties. Brown patties on both sides, place on a whole wheat bun, and top with top with barbecue sauce, Cheddar cheese, and, if desired, lettuce, tomato, and onion. Enjoy!

## How to Build the PERFECT Chicago Dog

The chef suggests making two because after the first you always crave one more!

### Ingredients

2   Ballpark Beef Franks
2   poppy seed hot dog buns
2   Tbsp. diced onion
2   Tbsp. neon-green relish
2   Tbsp. diced tomatoes
4   sport peppers
$^1/_2$   spear pickle
2   Tbsp. yellow mustard
    celery salt to taste

### Directions

**1.** Boil the hot dogs in 145 degree water per package instructions.

**2.** Remove from water and place each hot dog in its own bun.

**3.** Now comes the fun part: Load 1 Tbsp. relish down the dog and lay the pickle spear across from the relish. Place 1 Tbsp. each of tomato and onion on the same side down the length of the dog.

**4.** In authentic Windy City style, top the dog with yellow mustard, two sport peppers, and finish with celery salt. Enjoy, while cheering on the Cubbies!

**Remember: No ketchup, EVER!**

# Levy Restaurants

## Levy Restaurants Signature Crab Cakes with Lemon Aïoli

Serves 4

### Ingredients

1 lb. lump crab meat
1/2 cup panko bread crumbs
1/4 cup minced onion
1/4 cup butter, melted
1/4 cup minced celery
   salt to taste
   pepper to taste
1/4 cup lemon aïoli,
   recipe below

### Directions

**1.** Sauté the onions and celery in half of the butter until translucent. Let cool to room temperature.

**2.** Drain the crab meat, remove all shells, add to a bowl, and toss with the half of the lemon aïoli, bread crumbs, celery, and onion. Season with salt and pepper and form into 4 oz. patties.

**3.** Heat the remaining butter in a sauté pan and add the crab cake patties. Sauté for 3 minutes, or until golden brown, and turn over cake. Sauté for an additional 3 minutes, or until golden brown.

**4.** Place the crab cakes on a platter with three dollops of lemon aïoli on the side.

## Lemon Aïoli

### Ingredients

1 cup mayonnaise
1 pinch cayenne pepper
   juice of 1 lemon
1 tsp. lemon zest
1 tsp. minced garlic
   salt to taste

### Directions

**1.** Juice and zest the lemon.

**2.** Combine all the ingredients in a small bowl and mix well. Season with cayenne and salt to taste.

LEADING OFF

# Appetizers

When he's not playing baseball, *Mike Fontenot* disappears. "Usually in the off-season, you can't get a hold of me because I'm in the woods," the Cubs second baseman said. "I do a lot of duck and deer hunting in the off-season." He discovered this recipe while attending a football game at his alma mater, Louisiana State University. "The first time I had it was when I was tailgating in Baton Rouge," Fontenot said. "Somebody said, 'Try this.'" It's a popular way to eat duck or any game. "I've heard a lot of people say they do this," Fontenot said. "You can do it with a lot of stuff. Just wrap it in bacon. You can do this with deer meat, too." Of course, anything wrapped in bacon tastes good.

## Bacon-Wrapped Duck Breast

### Ingredients

2 or 3 duck breasts
   cut up banana peppers or jalapeño peppers
1   8 oz. package cream cheese
1   16 oz. package bacon
   toothpicks

### Directions

1. Cut the duck breast into bite-sized pieces.

2. Lay out one piece of bacon and put one piece of duck on one end of the strip.

3. Add a dab of cream cheese on top of the duck, then place either a banana pepper or jalapeño pepper (whichever you prefer, Fontenot says) on top.

4. Roll the piece of bacon up, starting at the end with the duck/cheese/pepper until the duck is wrapped.

5. Stick a toothpick through the bacon and duck to hold it together.

6. Repeat the process for each piece of duck until you are done.

7. Put the wrapped duck on the grill and cook until the bacon is done.

# Rudy Jaramillo

*spent 15 seasons with the Texas Rangers, and his wife, Shelley, was very involved with fundraising activities and community events. She deserves credit for some of the ideas in this cookbook project—and probably would've written the entire thing if given the chance. Thanks, Shelley, and thanks for sharing this popular family recipe, which comes from Rudy's cousin, Sydney.*

## Baked Herbed Cream Cheese en Croute or Mock Baked Brie

### Ingredients

- 4 crescent rolls (canned and refrigerated dough)
- 1 8 oz. package of cream cheese
- 2 Tbsp. garlic, minced
- 2 Tbsp. prepared pesto
- 2 Tbsp. chopped sun-dried tomatoes

### Directions

1. Preheat oven to 375 degrees.

2. Unroll crescent roll dough. Do not separate rolls. Pat seams to create one large square of dough.

3. Slice cream cheese horizontally, creating a "top" and "bottom." Place the bottom cream cheese diagonally on dough. Layer on the garlic, pesto, and tomatoes. Top with the other piece of cream cheese. Fold the crescent dough over the entire cream cheese loaf. Pinch the edges together so the cream cheese is entirely encased.

4. Place on cookie sheet sprayed with nonstick spray. Bake for 30 minutes or until dough is cooked and golden brown.

5. Remove with spatula and place on a small serving platter. Serve with your favorite crackers or bagel crisps.

*Country boy* **Randy Wells** *likes to make this dish whenever friends gather to watch a game, no matter if it's baseball or football. As for the proper order of ingredients on top of the chicken, he says: "It doesn't matter how you layer it." This is an easy dish to make and perfect if you're home watching a Cubs game. "It's one of my favorites," Randy said. "It's good Sunday football food." The way Randy sees it, most people eat chicken wings and have dip at their football parties. "This way," he says, "it combines both."*

## Randy Wells' Hot Wing Dip

Serves 4

### Ingredients

1 lb. chicken breasts boiled, then shredded
8 oz. ranch dressing
8 oz. cream cheese
8 oz. hot wing sauce
8 oz. shredded cheese of choice

### Directions

**1.** Preheat oven to 350 degrees.

**2.** Spread the cooked, shredded chicken in a nonstick baking dish. Layer the other ingredients on top. Randy begins with the shredded cheese, then the ranch dressing, then the hot sauce. Place dollops of cream cheese on top.

**3.** Bake for 15 minutes, then stir. By that point, the cream cheese has softened and it's easier to mix with other ingredients.

**4.** Bake for another 15 minutes and let sit. Eat with a strong tortilla chip.

PINCH HITTERS

*Sides*

*Imagine trying to make 30 guys happy at meal time with enough variety that they don't carry any stomach pangs onto the field. It's a tough assignment for Tom "Otis" Hellman, his brother Tim, and Gary Stark, who run the Cubs home clubhouse. The 2010 season marked the addition of a beautiful new kitchen, and the three prepped by attending a cooking boot camp with team nutritionist Dawn Jackson Blatner. For three days, six hours a day, they made more than 50 recipes to learn how to use healthy ingredients. These mashed potatoes are a huge favorite among the Cubs. As Gary says, "Guys are crushing them." That's a good thing.*

## Cubs Clubhouse: Yogurt Mashed Potatoes

Serves 6–8

### Ingredients

- 4   potatoes
- 4   Tbsp. plain low-fat Greek yogurt
- $1/2$ cup low sodium chicken broth
-     salt and pepper to taste

### Directions

**1.** Boil whole potatoes in pot of water. Reduce heat, cover, and simmer 45 minutes until tender.

**2.** Drain potatoes.

**3.** With masher, mash the potatoes and yogurt. Add the broth slowly, until desired consistency is reached.

**4.** Season with salt and pepper.

This is *John Grabow*'s idea of comfort food. The lefty likes to eat his version of mashed potatoes in the winter, most often at the holidays. "It's pretty easy to make," Grabow said, then cautions, "It's not very good for you." We'll make an exception for anything with bacon. Does Grabow cook a lot? "I do," he said. "My wife [Karey] is starting to cook more. She's starting to go outside the box." Grabow is not only comfortable on the mound but also using a grill. "Most guys stay out of the kitchen and like to barbeque," Grabow said. "I like to grill."

## John Grabow's Loaded Mashed Potatoes

Serves 8–10

### Ingredients

| | |
|---|---|
| 10–15 | red potatoes |
| 2–3 | tsp. of garlic powder |
| 5 | slices of cooked bacon |
| 2–3 | tsp. of salt |
| 1 to 1½ | cups of milk |
| 5 | Tbsp. of butter |
| 1–2 | cups of shredded Cheddar cheese |

### Directions

**1.** Boil the potatoes until soft. Mash the potatoes with a masher until the lumps are gone.

**2.** While potatoes are boiling, cook bacon. Drain and chop the bacon into small pieces.

**3.** Mix the milk and butter into the potatoes.

**4.** Mix the salt, garlic, and bacon into the potatoes.

**5.** Add the cheese and stir it all together.

In *Pat Hughes*' *back yard, the Cubs radio broadcaster has a little garden, tended to primarily by his wife, Trish. They grow tomatoes, cucumbers, and other healthy options that aren't always available in the media dining room at the many ballparks Pat visits. The WGN Radio play-by-play man said he and Trish are trying to eat healthier, so here's a perfect option for a summer day. In fact, the grilled aspara-gus is so good, Pat says he usually cooks a little too much and saves it for the next day's lunch.*

## Grilled Asparagus with Garlic

Serves 4

### Ingredients

1–2 bunches of asparagus (amount will depend on people you're serving)

10 cloves fresh garlic, peeled and coarsely chopped

1/2 fresh lemon

1–2 Tbsp. olive oil

### Directions

**1.** Prepare the asparagus. Rinse the spears and cut off the ends where the spears naturally break when bent. Put the spears in a bowl and mix with the olive oil, making sure the spears are completely covered with the oil.

**2.** Add the chopped garlic and mix thoroughly. Arrange the spears in a grilling basket and place next to the salmon on the hot grill.

**3.** Grill, turning the spears once, under tender-crisp, about 2–4 minutes. Remove from grill and put on a warmed platter. Squeeze the fresh lemon evenly over the asparagus.

Remember Crock-Pots? *Len Kasper*'s mom, Sharon, found this recipe more than 20 years ago when slow cookers were the rage. "It tasted just like my mother's recipe, which she never wrote down," Sharon Kasper said. "I have been using it ever since." Len is on the road from March until early October to broadcast the Cubs games on television. When he can head home to Michigan to be with his family for the holidays, this stuffing is always on the menu. "Len always says, the best thing about Thanksgiving is the leftovers, so I always make a lot," Sharon said.

## Mother Kasper's Slow-Cooker Stuffing

Serves 16

### Ingredients

- 1 cup butter, melted
- 2 cups chopped celery
- 1 cup chopped onion
- 1 tsp. poultry seasoning
- 1 1/2 tsp. sage
- 1/2 tsp. pepper
- 1 1/2 tsp. salt
- 1 tsp. thyme
- 2 eggs, beaten
- 4 cups chicken broth
- 12 cups dry bread crumbs

### Directions

**1.** Mix all ingredients in the order given.

**2.** Cook in a 4-quart slow cooker on high for 45 minutes, then reduce to low for 6 hours.

# Greg Maddux

*spent a lot of time in Chicago as a pitcher for the Cubs, beginning in 1986. Since then, he's won 355 games, four Cy Young Awards, 18 Gold Gloves, and raised a family with his wife, Kathy. Maddux retired from the game after the 2008 season but rejoined the Cubs in 2010 as an assistant to the general manager. He now offers advice to minor leaguers, sharing some insights and a few jokes. Whenever he's in Chicago, one of Greg's favorite stops is Rosebud Steakhouse on Walton. "That's our family place," Maddux said of the restaurant. "I'd crush a steak, my daughter would have the fried chicken, and my kid has pasta." Daughter, Amanda, and son, Chase, a.k.a. "the kid," also help Greg and Kathy devour these potatoes. Keep in mind, Rosebud believes in large portions.*

## Rosebud Restaurants—Chef Brito's Jalapeño Hash Browns

Serves 1

### Ingredients

- 2 Yukon Gold potatoes
- 1/2 Spanish onion
- 1/2 fresh jalapeno
- 2 Tbsp. Parmesan cheese
- 2 tsp. clarified butter

### Directions

**1.** Wash and scrub potatoes. Cut into half-inch cubes, leaving the skin on.

**2.** In a large pot of boiling water, cook the potatoes for 8 to 10 minutes. Drain and let dry.

**3.** In a deep fryer, fry the potatoes at 350 degrees until golden brown, about 2–3 minutes. Season with salt and pepper.

**4.** While the potatoes are cooking, dice the onion to the same size as the potatoes and sauté in 1 tsp. clarified butter until just soft and translucent.

**5.** Slice the jalapeno thinly, reserve. If you don't want it too hot, remove the seeds and ribs.

**6.** Toss all the ingredients together with the remaining 1 tsp. clarified butter and Parmesan cheese. Serve immediately.

**Note:** Pan-frying is an option for the potatoes if you don't have deep fryer. After cooking the potatoes in water and letting them dry, add 2 Tbsp. clarified butter to a sauté pan and heat on medium-high heat. Add the potatoes and pan-fry until golden brown, about 5–7 minutes. Season with salt and pepper.

Rosebud Restaurants
1419 W. Diversey Pky, Chicago, IL
(773)325-9700
rosebudrestaurants.com

For **Dave Keller**, one of the best things about having the Cubs spend Spring Training in Mesa, Arizona, is the chance to dine at the Blue Adobe Grille. The restaurant, on Country Club Road about a 10-minute drive from the team's facility, is busiest when Cactus League play begins. The Cubs take advantage of its proximity and quality New Mexican cuisine. Dave Keller, the team's Minor League hitting coordinator, has an edge over some of the others because he's in Mesa for more than just spring training but also instructional league and during the Arizona Fall League. You can find him at Blue Adobe at least once a week, and usually more often. "The Blue Adobe is a perfect complement to a great day—muy bueno," Keller said. Here's one of the restaurant's specialties. The serving size depends on the size of the chilies.

## Blue Adobe Grille Green Chile Potato

Serves 24

### Ingredients

- 24 Anaheim green chilies
- 4 lbs. potatoes
- 1/8 cup heavy cream
- 2 Tbsp. garlic puree
- 2 Tbsp. chipotle puree
- 1/8 lb. butter
- 1/2 cup red chilies
  pinch white pepper
  salt to taste

### Directions

1. Blister, peel, and remove seeds from chilies. Set aside.

2. Bake potatoes until tender.

3. Scoop out potato, discard skins.

4. Whip together all ingredients. Pipe into prepared chilies.

**CAUTION:** Wear gloves when handling chili peppers to avoid skin and eye irritation.

**Restaurant - Tavern**

**The Best Ribs Since 1932**

# *Alan Trammell* made his major

league debut at the age of 19 with Detroit and spent his entire 20-year playing career with the Tigers. He managed the Tigers from 2003–2005, and joined Lou Piniella's staff as the bench coach in 2007. What does a bench coach do? Besides organizing workouts and making out the lineup card, Trammell is a sounding board for Lou in the dugout. He can't simply be a "yes" man but has to be honest with the Cubs skipper to help make the right decision. As for food, Trammell has his favorites, and one of them is Twin Anchors Restaurant in Chicago. We tried to get the recipe to their famous ribs but the restaurant wouldn't reveal the secret. Instead, here's a side dish that should be an easy decision to make.

## Twin Anchors Restaurant & Tavern Pepper Jack Creamed Spinach

Serves 8–10

### Ingredients

- 4–5 lbs. fresh spinach, washed (not baby spinach)
- 1 yellow onion, finely chopped
- 2 Tbsp. vegetable oil
- 2 Tbsp. Worcestershire sauce
- 1 tsp. garlic powder
- 1/2 tsp. dried parsley
- 1/2 tsp. black pepper
- 1/2 tsp. celery salt
- 1 tsp. chopped jalapeño peppers (or to taste)
- 1/4 tsp. fresh red pepper, chopped
- 1 lb. Monterrey Jack cheese, shredded
- 8–12 oz. heavy cream or evaporated milk

### Directions

1. Clean and chop spinach, remove stems.

2. Blanch spinach in boiling water until cooked, approximately 3–5 minutes.

3. Drain and press through colander with towels to remove all liquid.

4. Chop onions and sauté in oil on medium heat, stirring frequently, until golden.

5. Add spinach and heat through on low heat.

6. Add jalapeños, then add all seasonings and stir well.

7. Add cheese and stir on low heat until melted through.

8. Add cream in small amounts to achieve desired smooth and creamy consistency. Serve immediately.

Twin Anchors Restaurant & Tavern
1655 N. Sedgwick St., Chicago, IL
(312) 266-1616
twinanchorsribs.com

*Very popular with* Carlos Zambrano *and Carlos Silva is the Venezuelan national dish* pabellon, *which is a combination of shredded beef, rice, and stewed black beans, often served with sweet plantains. When they get a craving for home-cooked food in spring training, they head to My Arepa in Mesa, Arizona. Restaurant owner Moises Mendez provided this recipe for black beans. We've provided the English and Spanish translation for the ingredients.*

## My Arepa Caraotas Black Beans

Serves 10–12

### Ingredients

- 2 lbs. black beans (caraotas)
- 5 garlic cloves (ajos)
- 1 onion (cebolla)
- 1 red pepper (pimenton rojo)
- 1 green pepper (pimenton verde)
- 3 green onions (ramitas de cebollin)
- 6 cilantro sprigs (ramitas de cilantro)
- 6 fresh parsley sprigs (ramitas de perejil)
- 3 mini sweet peppers (ajices dulces)
- 2 Tbsp. Worcestershire sauce (de salsa inglesa)
- 3 Tbsp. chicken base (de sazonador para pollo)
- $1/2$ tsp. cumin (pizca de comino)
- 1 Tbsp. canola oil
- pinch of salt (sal al gusto)

### Directions

**1.** Pick through and rinse the beans. Cook in simmering water for 2 hours until soft.

**2.** To make the sofrito (seasoned sauce), mince garlic, onion, peppers, green onions, and herbs into small pieces.

**3.** Add canola oil to a sauté pan and heat. Cook onions and peppers until softened. Add garlic and herbs for 30 seconds or until fragrant.

**4.** Add Worcestershire sauce and cumin, cook for a few minutes and add the chicken base. Cook and stir the mixture for a few minutes and then add it to the pot of beans.

**5.** Simmer for about 20 minutes.

Give *Jeff Baker*'s mom credit for this recipe. "Most of the time, my cooking is 90 seconds then push 'Start' on the microwave," he said. "I eat out a lot." He would have dinner with his family every Sunday after church and this is one of his favorite recipes. He admits that he's never made this chicken dish. "I couldn't cook that to save my life," Baker said. "This is my mom's." The Cubs infielder does eat healthy and has no problem finding the right stuff when he's eating out. "Everything's changed the last five, six, seven, eight years," he said. "Now, in restaurants you can go out and get chicken without all the stuff on it or order some nice fish. It's not as hard as it used to be. You don't want to be that guy who's asking about everything that's on the meat or ask the staff to put stuff on the side. There are a lot of healthy alternatives. It's not that hard, especially in Chicago where there are a lot of great places to eat."

## Jeff Baker's Mom's Chicken Cordon Bleu

Serves 6

### Ingredients

- 6 medium whole chicken breasts, skinned and boned
- 3 Tbsp. flour
- 1 tsp. paprika
- 6 Tbsp. butter or margarine
- 1/2 cup dry white wine or water
- 1 8 oz. package Swiss cheese slices
- 1 8 oz. package cooked ham slices
- 1 chicken bouillon cube
- 1 Tbsp. cornstarch
- 1 cup heavy or whipping cream

### Directions

**1.** Spread the chicken breasts flat. Fold the cheese and ham slices to fit on one half of chicken breast.

**2.** Fold the other half of the chicken breast over the top and fasten edges together with toothpicks.

**3.** On waxed paper, mix the flour and paprika. Use this to coat chicken pieces.

**4.** Melt the butter or margarine in a large skillet over medium heat.

**5.** Cook the chicken until browned on all sides. Add wine (or water) and bouillon.

**6.** Reduce heat to low. Cover and simmer 30 minutes or until fork tender. Remove the toothpicks.

**7.** In a cup, blend the cornstarch and cream until smooth. Gradually stir into the skillet.

**8.** Cook, stirring constantly, until thickened. Serve the sauce over the chicken.

*Pitcher* **Mike Bielecki** *had his best season in 1989 with the Cubs, winning 18 games, third most in the National League, and helping the team win the Eastern Division. The right-hander spent four of his 14 seasons in Chicago and is a regular at the Cubs Convention in January. Here's a recipe that has a little kick to it. The chef testing this dish suggested cooking the ginger in the wok with the vegetables and half the scallions because raw ginger can be a little overpowering. That's what opponents said about Mike's fastball back in '89, too.*

## Protein Thai Noodles

Serves 4–6

### Ingredients

- 1 lb. box whole wheat ziti (or preferred pasta)
- 1 cup creamy peanut butter
- 2 Tbsp. fresh ginger root, chopped fine
- 2 Tbsp. soy sauce (can add teriyaki with soy)
- 2 cups frozen string beans or snow peas
- 1 cup red pepper, cut in strips
- 3 stalks scallions (spring onions), chopped
- canola oil for stir-frying
- 2–3 boneless chicken breasts (optional), cut in diced into cubes

### Directions

**1.** For dish with chicken, add a little canola oil and soy or teriyaki sauce to wok or fry pan and heat over medium-high heat. If desired, sprinkle in some sesame seeds. Stir-fry chicken until opaque (about 3 minutes) and set aside. (Skip this step for vegetarian recipe.)

**2.** In a separate bowl, mix ginger, soy sauce, teriyaki, and peanut butter.

**3.** Cook pasta according to package directions. During the last 3 minutes, add beans or snow peas and red pepper. Drain, saving $^1/_2$ cup of the water, and set aside.

**4.** Stir-fry vegetables by adding 1 Tbsp. canola oil to a wok or frying pan, add 1 Tbsp. ginger and half the scallions, cook 30 seconds. Add veggies and cook for about 2–3 minutes. Add to drained pasta.

**5.** Reheat $^1/_2$ cup of pasta water to boiling and add to bowl with the ginger, soy, teriyaki, and peanut butter. Mix to create a sauce.

**6.** Place pasta and veggies in a large bowl and add the chicken. Pour the sauce over the noodles and mix well. Sprinkle the chopped scallions on top to finish.

ITALIAN STEAKHOUSE & BAR

*Ernie Banks'* favorite place in Chicago is Wrigley Field. That's why he's Mr. Cub. His second favorite place could be Harry Caray's restaurant. "Since coming back to live in Chicago, there's no place I've spent more time than Harry's," Ernie said of the restaurant, named after the legendary Cubs broadcaster. "It's such a welcoming place, and the food is great. The Navy Pier location is beautiful, and I love hanging out there and talking to the fans." Ernie's favorite dish at Harry Caray's Tavern Navy Pier is the Tallgrass Meatloaf. Not only does it taste like a meal fit for a Hall of Famer but it's made with Bill Kurtis' grass-fed Tallgrass Beef, which is delicious and healthy. Maybe you should cook up two?

## Harry Caray's Tallgrass Meatloaf

Serves 8

### Ingredients

5 lbs. grass-fed Tallgrass Beef or extra lean ground beef
2 1/2 lbs. ground sausage
1/2 lb. diced red bell pepper
1/2 lb. diced yellow bell pepper
1 1/4 oz. diced jalapeno
1 lb. diced onion
25 roasted garlic cloves
1/4 loaf white bread, cubed
1 cup veal stock
4 eggs
4 oz. Dijon mustard
6 oz. ketchup
1/2 tsp. black pepper
1/4 tsp. kosher salt
Parmesan cheese to cover
Swiss cheese slices to cover

### Directions

**1.** Preheat oven to 350 degrees.

**2.** In a sauté pan, combine olive oil and shelled garlic and cook until soft. Add red and yellow bell peppers, onion, and jalapeno to pan. Sauté vegetables in oil until softened but still crunchy.

**3.** Toss bread in eggs and veal stock, folding lightly until majority of the liquid is absorbed.

**4.** Mix all ingredients together and place in loaf pan. Cook in oven until internal temperature of the loaf reaches 155 degrees. Top loaf with Swiss and Parmesan cheeses and bake until melted.

**5.** Remove from oven, slice, and serve.

Harry Caray's Chicago
33 W. Kinzie St., Chicago, IL 60610
(773) HOLY-COW
harrycarays.com

# *Marlon Byrd*'s wife, Andrea, is Ukranian, Irish, English, and Italian, which means she can provide a lot of variety for the family meals. This recipe is from her Italian side, Marlon said. One thing the Byrds do emphasize is using organic ingredients. They believe it's healthier and tastier. Does Marlon cook? "I do meats," he said. "I can do anything with meats." At home, Andrea does the majority of the cooking. One constant Marlon developed while with the Texas Rangers was to eat bacon, egg, and cheese on an English muffin with avocado every morning. And now that he's with the Cubs and they play day games? "Bacon, egg, and cheese on an English muffin with avocado—just a little earlier," Marlon said.

## Marlon & Andrea Byrd's Baked Ziti

Serves 6–8

### Ingredients

- 1   16 oz. box ziti pasta
- 3¹/₂ cups spaghetti sauce
- 2   cups whole ricotta cheese
- 2   cups fresh mozzarella packed in water, separated (shred it yourself, making the finished ziti creamier than with packaged shredded cheese)
- 1   egg slightly beaten
- ¹/₄ tsp. nutmeg
- ¹/₄ cup chopped fresh parsley
- 1   tsp. oregano
- ¹/₂ tsp. garlic powder
- ¹/₄ tsp. pepper
- 1   Tbsp. grated Parmesan cheese
-     nonstick cooking spray

### Directions

1. Preheat oven to 375 degrees.

2. Cook ziti according to package (add a pinch of salt and teaspoon of extra virgin olive oil to water before boiling) and drain.

3. In a large bowl, mix ricotta cheese and nutmeg. Next, add egg, 1¹/₂ cups of the mozzarella cheese, parsley, oregano, garlic powder, and pepper. Mix well.

4. Add 1¹/₂ cups spaghetti sauce and the cooked ziti. Mix well.

5. Spray a 9″ x 13″ pan lightly with cooking spray. Pour ¹/₂ cup of the spaghetti sauce. Spread the ziti mixture evenly over the sauce.

6. Top with remaining 1¹/₂ cups spaghetti sauce and spread evenly. Top that with the remaining shredded mozzarella cheese and sprinkle with Parmesan cheese.

7. Bake covered for 30–35 minutes or until hot and bubbly.

This is comfort food for *Andrew Cashner*. The right-hander, who was the Cubs' No. 1 draft pick in June 2008, got the recipe from a relative. "My mom makes it all the time," Cashner said. "It's my favorite thing to eat." These aren't big meatballs, like the ones you see in spaghetti, but smaller. Cashner is working on getting to the big leagues—and on some other recipes. "I do like to cook," he said.

## Grandma Pat's Meatballs

Serves 6–8

### Ingredients

- 1 lb. ground beef
- ¼ cup milk
- ⅓ cup bread crumbs (fine)
- 1 tsp. salt
- ½ tsp. black pepper
- 1 medium onion, finely chopped
- 1 medium potato, grated on a large grater (about 2 cups)
- 1-2 Tbsp. oil
- 1 10¾ oz. can cream of mushroom soup

### Directions

1. Preheat oven to 350 degrees.

2. Mix the above ingredients together in a bowl.

3. Mold the mix into balls, about the size of a golf ball.

4. Put 1-2 Tbsp. of oil in a pan and brown the meatballs over medium heat.

5. Place meatballs in a baking dish and cover with cream of mushroom soup.

6. Bake for 30–40 minutes.

After the 2009 season, the Cubs gave *Tyler Colvin* a choice. The young outfielder could play in Mexico and get more at-bats or he could spend the off-season in Arizona with strength coach Tim Buss. Colvin chose the latter. He added 25 pounds of good weight, built up his strength and endurance, and all of his hard work showed when he arrived for spring training. He led the majors with a .468 batting average in Cactus League play. What does that have to do with food? Tyler didn't live on fattening cheeseburgers or chocolate cake. With the help of his fiancé, Molly, Tyler ate right and ate smart. This casserole recipe was one of his favorites. When she was first asked to submit a recipe for this cookbook, Molly provided one for cucumber finger sandwiches. Tyler nixed that. It's good if you're having tea in the afternoon. This casserole could help you hit home runs.

## Molly's Chicken Broccoli Casserole

Serves 6–8

### Ingredients

- 8 cups fresh or frozen broccoli florets
- 8 skinless boneless chicken breast halves
- 1 $10^3/4$ oz. can cream of chicken soup
- $1^1/4$ cups milk
- 1 cup shredded Cheddar cheese
- $1/4$ cup dry bread crumbs
- 2 Tbsp. butter, melted

### Directions

1. Preheat oven to 350 degrees.

2. Arrange broccoli and chicken in a 4-quart shallow, greased baking dish.

3. Stir soup and milk together in a small bowl, and pour over the broccoli and chicken.

4. Sprinkle the cheese over the mixture. Mix the bread crumbs with the butter and sprinkle over the tops.

5. Bake for 45 minutes or until chicken is cooked through.

*Tomato broth blended with sausage, pepperoni, and pizza dough. Garnished with pizza crisps and mozzarella cheese.*

## Pizza Soup

### Ingredients

- 8 oz. onions
- 2 lb. Roma tomatoes
- 1 oz. fresh basil
- 1 tsp. dried oregano
- 1 tsp. fresh minced garlic
- 1 qt. pizza sauce
- 4 oz. sausage
- 4 oz. pepperoni
- 4 oz. red wine
- 2 oz. sugar
- 4 oz. butter
- 4 oz. heavy cream
- 4 oz. olive oil
- 1 tsp. parsley
- 2 tsp. salt
- 4 oz. chopped pizza crust
- $^1/_4$ tsp. chili flanks
- $1^1/_2$ qt. chicken stock

### Directions

**1.** Bake the onions, Roma tomatoes, 2 oz. of the olive oil, and fresh basil for 45 minutes at 450 degrees.

**2.** In a large saucepan, cook the pepperoni and sausage in the remaining 2 oz. of olive oil for 8 minutes.

**3.** Add the baked onions, Roma tomatoes, and fresh basil to the pan and cook for another 5 minutes.

**4.** Pour the red wine into the mixture and cook for another 5 minutes.

**5.** Add the pizza sauce, chicken stock, sugar, and the chopped pizza crust and cook for 30 minutes.

**6.** Add the butter, cream, and chili flanks and blend all together until completely pureed.

**7.** Serve garnished with shredded mozzarella cheese, pizza crisps, and parsley.

Connie's Pizza
2373 S. Archer Ave., Chicago, IL, 60616
(312) 326-3443
conniespizza.com

This is a recipe Cubs coach *Ivan DeJesus* loved as a child in Puerto Rico and is something his wife, Martha, makes. Think of it as a Latin variation of lasagna. "Other people do this but use different ingredients," Ivan said. When you go shopping for plantains, you will likely find green ones and yellow ones. The green one is hard and is a little dry. Ivan recommends using the yellow, sweet plantain. "It's like a banana—you can buy it when it's green but it will turn yellow," he said. Plus, it's softer. Ivan does cook himself. "I like to cook salmon—that's my fish," he said. "I do that real well. I do it on a fry pan, no oil or nothing, just a little seasoning." Is he a good cook? "I try to be," DeJesus said. "I'm trying to learn."

## Pastelon de Amarillos (Ripe Plantains Lasagna)

Serves 8–10

### Ingredients

- 2 Tbsp. olive oil
- 3 garlic cloves
- 1/2 cup olives
- 2 green bell peppers, chopped
- 1/2 medium onion, chopped
- 3 bay leaves
- 2 Tbsp. cooking wine
- 1/2 lb. lean ground meat
- 1/3 cup raisins
- 6 ripe plantains (amarillos)
- 2 Tbsp. olive oil
- 3 Tbsp. melted butter
- 3 eggs, beaten
- 1 Tbsp. grated Parmesan cheese

### Directions

1. Preheat oven to 350 degrees.

2. Pour 2 Tbsp. olive oil in a medium saucepan and heat over medium heat. Add the first six ingredients (cloves, olives, peppers, onion, bay leaves, wine) and sauté for about 5 minutes.

3. Stir the ground meat into the ingredients in the saucepan. Cook for about 10 minutes. Add the raisins. Continue to cook for another 10 minutes or until the meat is cooked but not dry. You may want to remove the bay leaves at this time.

4. Slice the plantains lengthwise. Use a separate saucepan to fry the plantain slices over medium heat in 2 Tbsp. of olive oil. Remove from saucepan. Wipe the excess oil off with paper napkins.

5. Use a deep, square baking pan. Grease thoroughly with about half of the melted butter. Cover the bottom of the pan with a row of plantains. Add enough of the cooked meat mixture to make a layer, following the style for preparing lasagna. Alternate rows of plantains and meat until both are used up.

6. Pour the remaining melted butter and the beaten eggs over the mixture. Sprinkle with Parmesan cheese.

7. Bake for about 20 minutes.

Whenever *Ryan Dempster* pitches in Chicago for the Cubs, he eats D'Agostino's grilled chicken Parmesan. "That's always my pregame meal," Ryan said of the dish. "The night before, I always have chicken Parmesan and some mostaccioli with marinara sauce." There are four D'Agostino's locations in the Chicago area, but Ryan stops by the one closest to Wrigley Field. There must be a good vibe there. D'Agostinos also supports the Dempster Foundation by donating $1 for every pizza purchased on the 22nd of each month. So check the Cubs pitching schedule and try this dish the night before Ryan starts.

## D'Agostino's Grilled Chicken Parmesan

Serves 5

### Ingredients

- 5   boneless chicken breasts, pounded to 1/2 inch thick
- 1   Tbsp. minced garlic
- 1/2  cup olive oil
- 8   slices mozzarella cheese
     DAGS Marinara Sauce (see below)
     Parmesan cheese
     spaghetti or French bread

### Directions

**1.** Preheat oven to 350 degrees.

**2.** Marinate chicken in oil and garlic. Char-grill the chicken on both sides until golden on each side. Place chicken in a greased baking dish.

**3.** Pour sauce over all. Place two pieces of mozzarella cheese on each chicken breast.

**4.** Sprinkle with Parmesan cheese.

**5.** Bake for about 12 to 15 minutes or until cheese is melted.

**6.** Serve on a bed of spaghetti or on French bread for a sandwich.

D'Agostinos
1351 W. Addison St., Chicago, IL
(773) 477-1821
dagostinospizza.com

### DAGS Marinara Ingredients

- 5   Tbsp. extra virgin olive oil
- 4   cloves garlic, sliced
- 1/3  cup chopped white onion
- 1   cup water
- 2   tsp. salt
- 2   tsp. black pepper
- 2   tsp. white sugar
- 6   oz. tomato paste
- 6   oz. tomato puree
- 12  oz. plum tomatoes
- 1   tsp. oregano
- 6   leaves fresh basil leaves, torn

### Directions

**1.** Heat oil in a large, nonstick skillet over low heat and sauté garlic and onion for about 2 minutes; be careful not to burn. Just as the garlic begins to turn brown, remove pan from heat.

**2.** Allow pan to cool. Add water, salt, pepper, sugar, paste, puree, and plum tomatoes. Cook over medium-high heat and bring to a boil.

**3.** Reduce heat to low. Add basil leaves and oregano. Cover and simmer for about 20 minutes.

*Ryan Dempster* loves to eat fish. When he's home, he'll grill salmon on his backyard grill. But when he's dining out in Chicago, Ryan heads for Hub 51 on West Hubbard Street. He orders this broiled sea bass every time. "It's unbelievable it's so good—all their food is good," Ryan said. "This is a phenomenal dish." Hub 51 also helped the Dempster Family Foundation by hosting the official launch party for Ryan and Jenny Dempster's efforts on January 17, 2010. Illinois governor Pat Quinn was among the guests, and the foundation raised $200,000 in the inaugural event. Try Ryan's favorite fish. It's for a good cause.

## HUB 51 Broiled Sea Bass in Horseradish Broth

Serves 4

### Ingredients

**Horseradish Broth**

- 3 cups water
- 1/2 cup fish sauce
- 2 Tbsp. rice wine vinegar
- 1 Tbsp. light soy sauce
- 2 tsp. palm sugar
- 1/2 cup rough chopped button mushrooms
- 2 tsp. rough chopped ginger
- 1 tsp. chopped lemongrass
- 1/4 cup Thai chili
- 1/4 cup kaffir lime leaves
- 1/2 cup peeled and grated fresh horseradish
- 1/2 lb. ice

**Fish**

- 4 7 oz. Chilean sea bass filets (skinned and boned)
  cooked barley (per box directions)
- 1/2 cup pea tendrils or spinach, cleaned and washed

### Directions

**1.** For the broth, whisk all ingredients together except ice and horseradish. Bring to a boil and add horseradish. Simmer for 15 minutes and strain. Add ice to cool down and dilute.

**2.** For the sea bass, sprinkle fish lightly with salt and pepper. Broil (or grill) until cooked through.

**3.** To serve, plate the fish in a shallow bowl on top of cooked barley. Pour warm horseradish broth over the fish, and garnish with pea tendrils.

HUB 51
51 W. Hubbard St., Chicago, IL
(312) 828-0051
hub51chicago.com

*The Fifty/50 Signature Skirt Steak Sandwich comes from an old hippie recipe that was passed on to me when I was a kid. My friend's parents used to follow the Grateful Dead on tour and in order to pay for travel and tickets they would buy grocery store skirt steak and marinate it overnight in teriyaki sauce, orange juice, and honey. I was always fond of this preparation, especially the way the natural sugars from the marinade would caramelize on the grill and create a great summertime aroma. At the Fifty/50 we buy hand-butchered, center-cut skirt steaks and make our signature honey, orange, and teriyaki glaze from scratch with fresh squeezed orange juice and fresh minced ginger.*

## The Fifty/50 Skirt Steak Sandwich

Serves 6

### Ingredients

- 6   8 oz. skirt steaks
- 10   cups Honey, Orange, Teriyaki Glaze (see right)
- 6   8-inch rustic Italian bread or ciabatta, sliced
- 1   cup garlic butter (see right)
- 1   medium red onion, thinly sliced
- 1/4   stick butter, unsalted
- 4   Tbsp. kosher salt
- 2   Tbsp. cracked black pepper

### Honey, Orange, Teriyaki Glaze Ingredients

- 3   cups soy sauce
- 1   cup rice wine vinegar
- 1   cup peeled, minced fresh ginger
- 1   cup peeled, minced fresh garlic
- 1/4   cup toasted sesame seeds
- 1/3   cup pure clover honey
- 1/2   cup fresh-squeezed orange juice
- 1   lb. (1 package) dark brown sugar

### Garlic Butter Ingredients

- 1/2   lb. unsalted butter, softened
- 2   cloves peeled, minced fresh garlic
- 1   tsp. fresh chopped Italian parsley
- 1   Tbsp. extra virgin olive oil
- 1   tsp. kosher salt
- 1/2   tsp. cracked black pepper

### Directions

**1.** One day prior to serving, marinate the skirt steaks in the Honey, Orange, Teriyaki Glaze. (About 8–12 hours in the marinade is preferable.)

**2.** Preheat grill on high heat. Brush each bread roll with the garlic butter and lightly toast. Remove and plate.

**3.** Place red onion slices in foil pouch with the unsalted butter and any remaining garlic butter and place on grill.

**4.** Season each steak with kosher salt and cracked black pepper and place on grill. Cook to desired temperature and let rest off the heat for 3–5 minutes.

**5.** Remove onions from grill.

**6.** Place steaks on garlic bread and top with the sautéed onions.

### Honey, Orange, Teriyaki Glaze Directions

Whisk all ingredients together. Set aside 1 cup for basting during grilling.

### Garlic Butter Directions

**1.** Lightly sauté garlic in olive oil over medium heat. Just when first pieces of garlic begin to brown, add the butter.

**2.** Fold in chopped parsley, salt, and pepper. Set aside. Recipe can be made day prior to serving.

The Fifty/50
2047 W. Division St., Chicago, IL
(773) 489-5050
thefifty50.com

# Kosuke Fukudome

*may be playing in the U.S. major leagues but he's always looking for Japanese restaurants. Often, the Japanese sportswriters help him find places so he feels more at home. In spring training, Fukudome's interpreter Hiro Aoyama and athletic trainer Yoshi Nakazawa take turns making dinner. Finding the ingredients shouldn't be hard. What is tough, Aoyama said, is getting the meat sliced thin enough. Think very, very thin, like you'd find at a deli counter. Aoyama does have access to a meat slicer. Mirin is an essential Japanese condiment, similar to rice wine, and available in most grocery stores. The following is a fairly simple recipe that Aoyama likes to make—and Fukudome likes to eat. Aoyama says you can add some slices of white or yellow onions or bean sprouts to the mixture for added flavor and texture. Hiro's version is very salty, so be careful how much soy sauce you add. We've come up with another version that may be a little easier—and doesn't require a meat slicer.*

## Hiro Aoyama's Ginger Pork

Serves 4

### Ingredients

- 1 lb. thinly sliced pork loin
- 1 Tbsp. grated fresh ginger root
- 4 Tbsp. soy sauce
- 4 Tbsp. cooking sake
- 2 Tbsp. Mirin

### Directions

**1.** In a bowl, mix the sliced pork, ginger, soy sauce, sake, and Mirin.

**2.** Cover and marinate for at least a half hour. Heat a pan or wok and fry the mixture until cooked—the meat will turn brown.

**3.** Serve with rice, miso soup, and some sliced cabbage.

## Ginger Pork (lower salt)

### Ingredients

- 1 lb. pork loin chops, about two 8 oz. chops
- 1 Tbsp. grated fresh ginger root
- 2 Tbsp. soy sauce
- 4 Tbsp. sake
- 2 Tbsp. Mirin
- 1 head of Napa cabbage, sliced thin into strips
- 1 cup of jasmine rice, steamed
- 1-2 Tbsp. high heat oil like peanut or grapeseed for cooking pork

### Directions

**1.** Slice the loin chops into ¼-inch strips (the short way). For easier slicing, place chops in a freezer for 15 minutes.

**2.** In a non-reactive bowl or glass dish, mix ginger, soy sauce, sake, and Mirin.

**3.** Add pork, cover, and marinate in the refrigerator for a half hour.

**4.** Cook rice according to package directions.

**5.** Slice cabbage. Set aside.

**6.** Heat a sauté pan. Add 1–2 Tbsp. high-heat oil, like grapeseed or peanut oil, and sear the meat on one side.

**7.** Turn the meat, then add the rest of the marinade mixture. The meat will turn brown and the sauce will thicken.

**8.** Serve over the rice with the cabbage on the side.

*Jeff Gray* likes hamburgers. Actually, he loves hamburgers. But the Cubs reliever doesn't want to eat the same thing every day. His fiancée, Lisa, found this recipe and it was a winner. "It puts a little spice in things," Jeff said. As for the potatoes, Lisa surprised him with the sweet potato recipe. "She brought them to the table one day and said, 'Try these,'" Jeff said. "We always like a lot of the same food and we also like to try different things." The two do cook together. Usually, Jeff handles the grill and Lisa takes care of the rest. Did he ever help out his parents when growing up in Texas City, Texas? "No chance," Jeff said. "I was out playing too many sports at the time." Spoken like a ballplayer.

## Southwestern Turkey Burgers with Sweet Potato Fries

Serves 4

### Ingredients

**Turkey Burgers**

1¹⁄₃ lb. ground turkey

4 oz. can diced green chilies, drained

¹⁄₄ tsp. salt

¹⁄₄ tsp. black pepper

2–3 drizzles canola oil

3 oz. reduced fat pepper jack cheese

4 whole wheat Kaiser rolls

tomato

red onion

lettuce

¹⁄₂ avocado, sliced

**Sweet Potato Fries**

2 sweet potatoes

1 Tbsp. olive oil

¹⁄₂ tsp. chili powder

¹⁄₄ tsp. salt

juice from half a lime

### Directions

1. Preheat oven to 425 degrees.

2. Wash and dry potatoes. With skins on, slice into half-inch round slices and then cut into half-inch-thick pieces. Toss the potatoes in a bowl with the olive oil, chili powder, garlic powder, and salt.

3. Place the potatoes on a baking sheet and bake. Stir every 10 minutes until brown and tender, about 30–35 minutes.

4. In a large bowl, mix the turkey with the chilies and season with salt and pepper. Mold into patties.

5. Drizzle oil in a grill pan or nonstick skillet and heat over medium heat. Grill the patties until they're brown on one side (about 4 minutes). Flip and reduce the heat to low and cover. Cook until juice is pale pink (about 4 minutes). Top with the pepper jack cheese.

6. Toast the bun. Place a patty on the bun with a slice of onion, tomato, lettuce, and avocado. Spritz the fries with lime juice and serve.

# Pat Hughes *has spent more than 30 years broadcasting baseball games, beginning in 1978 with the San Jose Missions minor league team and eventually reaching Chicago and the Cubs. The 2010 season is Pat's 15th with WGN Radio and exuberant color man Ron Santo. And all those games on the road means Pat has eaten more than his share of room service and not-so-good-for-you food in media dining rooms. This salmon recipe is a favorite when Pat is home with his wife, Trish. "With all the traveling we do, it's really a treat to have a home-cooked meal," Pat said. "My wife is a great cook." Try it, and we're sure you'll call it a winner.*

## Caramelized Plank Salmon

Serves 4

### Ingredients

1½ lbs. fresh salmon filet, skin on

fresh mixed peppercorn blend or seasoned pepper blend

½ fresh lemon

½ Tbsp. brown sugar (packed firmly)

6 fresh garlic cloves, peeled and coarsely chopped

olive oil

1 cedar plank (about the same size as the filet)

### Directions

**1.** Prepare the cedar plank for grilling. Completely submerge the plank in cold water for at least 1 hour, preferably longer. (If you don't follow this step, the plank will burn.) When the plank is prepared correctly, the salmon will pick up a subtle cedar flavor. You can find the planks at most grocery stores.

**2.** After rinsing and drying the filet, brush the top with olive oil, squeeze the half lemon over the top, then sprinkle the freshly ground peppercorns over the filet, to taste. Next, evenly sprinkle on the fresh garlic. Sprinkle the brown sugar on top.

**3.** Once the grill is ready, place the prepared filet skin side down on the plank. Place plank directly on the grill grate. Cover grill and cook until the fish is opaque throughout and flakes when tested with a fork, about 8–10 minutes. Don't worry if the plank is slightly charred.

Do you want to make *Jim Hendry*, *Ryan Theriot, and Mike Fontenot, happy? Prepare some crawfish étouffée, a popular dish in New Orleans and the Louisiana bayou country. It's similar to gumbo. In French, the word étouffée literally means "smothered" or "suffocated." It's usually served over rice. Hendry's friend Vickie Courville, who grew up outside of New Orleans, provided this recipe. The seasoning can be any Cajun mix.*

## Crawfish Étouffée

Serves 4–6

### Ingredients

- 1   10³/₄ oz. can cream of mushroom soup
- 1   can diced tomatoes with green chili peppers
- 1   stick of butter
- 1   onion
- 1   bell pepper
- 3   stalks of celery
- 1   lb. peeled crawfish
      Cajun seasoning to taste

### Directions

**1.** In a 4-quart saucepan, sauté the onion and bell pepper in butter until soft.

**2.** Add the soup and tomatoes, and stir in the crawfish.

**3.** Simmer on medium heat for 45 minutes.

**4.** Season to taste with Cajun seasoning.

# Jim Hendry

*Jim Hendry eats out a lot on the road because of his travel schedule, but when he's home, he prefers Cajun cooking by his significant other, Vickie Courville. She learned how to cook from her mother while growing up in Lafayette, Louisiana, which is about two hours from New Orleans. It's tough to plan meals because of away games, last minute trades, and meetings so Vickie has learned a few tricks, such as making a huge pot of the gumbo and freezing it so when they come home, it's ready. It's also been tough to find good Cajun food in Chicago. "It's not the same," Vickie said of the restaurants she's tested. "Their gumbos have more of a red sauce. With a gumbo, you can make the roux from scratch or you can buy it in a jar. It's a long process to make your own roux. You have to constantly stir the flour to do it right. It smokes up the kitchen and you have to be prepared for all that." The roux (pronounced "roo") is the key. It's a thickener for soups and sauces, dating back more than 300 years in French cuisine. There is a low-fat version you can make without the oils. Just brown the flour and keep stirring it in a skillet. Vickie says some people will add a little olive oil or cooking oil. The process requires some TLC and a team effort to make it work. Says Vickie: "Everybody gathers in the kitchen when we're cooking."*

## Chicken and Sausage Gumbo

Serves 6

### Ingredients

- 1 cup all-purpose flour
- 2 large onions, chopped
- 1/2 cup vegetable oil
- 1 stalk celery, chopped
- 2 Tbsp. shortening
- 1 lb. smoked sausage, sliced
- 2 1/2 lb. broiler-fryer, cut up into 1/2-inch-thick chunks
- 1 large bell pepper, seeded and chopped
- 4 quarts water
   salt and pepper to taste
- 2 cups rice, cooked according to package directions

### Directions

**1.** Make a roux by slowly browning flour in vegetable oil over medium heat. This is a slow process, and the roux must be carefully watched and stirred constantly.

**2.** In another skillet, brown chicken in shortening.

**3.** Remove chicken. Sauté onion, bell pepper, and celery in skillet.

**4.** Combine all ingredients in 5-quart aluminum pot.

**5.** Cook over low heat for two hours or until chicken is tender, but not falling off the bone.

**6.** Serve over hot rice in a deep bowl.

*Meghan and* **Koyie Hill** *make this dish at least once a month. It's loaded with good-for-you ingredients. "We're healthy eaters," Koyie said. The recipe comes from Meghan and her mother's family and helps the Hills deal with winter in Kansas. "In Wichita, when it's freezing all the time, it's nice to have," Koyie said of the stew. The catcher was the Cubs' iron man in 2009 when he was behind the plate for 26 straight games. He's also able to handle quite a bit of the workload in the kitchen. "I'm the breakfast and lunch cook," Koyie said. "Meghan is the dinner cook, and there's not much she can't do. She's good." So who cleans up? "Both of us," Koyie said. The two like to check out recipes on the Internet for ideas. "It's usually a themed thing—like at the Super Bowl, you want chili or something," Koyie said. "We'll check and see if anybody out there has a different way of doing it." Here's their version of pork stew.*

## Koyie & Meghan Hill's Pork Stew

Serves 6–8

### Ingredients

- 2 Tbsp. olive oil
- 1 white onion, chopped
- 2 cloves garlic, chopped
- 1 large pork loin
- 1 49 oz. can chicken broth
- 6 zucchini, sliced
- 6 large potatoes, peeled and cubed
- 1 15 oz. can stewed tomatoes
- 3 cubes chicken bouillon
- 1 4 oz. can diced green chilies
- 1 small jar sliced jalapeños
- 2 cups shredded Cheddar cheese

### Directions

**1.** In a large stockpot, sauté the chopped onion and garlic in olive oil until the onion is transparent. Add the pork loin and cover in water. Bring to a boil, then simmer for approximately 2 hours. The pork is done when it can be shredded easily.

**2.** Once the pork is cooked, remove it from the broth and shred. Set aside.

**3.** Add chicken broth to the remaining water in the pot. Add the potatoes and zucchini. Cook medium heat until the potatoes and zucchini are tender. Turn heat to low and add the shredded pork back into the pot. Add the tomatoes and bouillon to taste.

**4.** When all ingredients are warm, ladle the soup into bowls and top each serving with shredded cheese, green chilies, and jalapeños.

**5.** Serve with warm tortillas.

## Build-Your-Own Steak Tacos

Serves 4

### Ingredients

- 4  6–8 oz. prime steaks of your choice (prefer filet mignon, rib eye, or skirt steak)
- 2  cups brown sugar
- 3  cups low-sodium soy sauce
- 1/8  cup Worcestershire sauce
- 2  tsp. hot pepper sauce
- 1  package corn tortillas
  Roasted Tomato Salsa (see right)
  Guacamole (see right)

### Directions

1. For marinade, combine brown sugar, soy sauce, Worcestershire sauce, and hot pepper sauce.

2. Place steaks in a pan; cover with marinade. Marinate steaks in a refrigerator for 1 to 2 hours. Drain off marinade and discard.

3. Cook steaks on high grill until cooked to desired temperature. Let steaks rest for 2 to 3 minutes and slice.

4. the sliced steak with tortillas (warmed), guacamole, roasted tomato salsa, and all other desired toppings and sides. Serve as build-your-own tacos.

### Roasted Tomato Salsa Ingredients

- 8  cups ripe Roma tomatoes
- 2  charred jalapeños
- 2  tsp. kosher salt
- 2  garlic cloves
- 1/2  tsp. ground black pepper
- 5  dried pasilla peppers
- 3  chipotle peppers in adobo
- 2  tsp. fresh lime juice
- 4  cups arugula, cleaned
- 3/4  cup fresh chopped cilantro

### Roasted Tomato Salsa Directions

1. De-stem tomatoes and slice in half.

2. Broil tomatoes and jalapeños skin side up until brown and blistered. Allow to cool.

3. Rehydrate pasilla peppers in warm water for 15 minutes, then drain.

4. Place all ingredients except cilantro in a blender and blend until very smooth. Fold in chopped cilantro and serve.

### Guacamole Ingredients

- 1  avocado
- 1  tsp. finely diced yellow onion
- 1  Tbsp. diced tomato
- 1  tsp. minced jalapeño
- 1  Tbsp. lime juice
- 1  Tbsp. chopped cilantro
  salt to taste

### Guacamole Directions

1. Mash the avocado with the remaining ingredients in a small bowl.

### Optional Toppings and Sides

pico de gallo

rice

beans

chopped cilantro

sour cream

HUB 51
51 W. Hubbard St., Chicago, IL
(312) 828-0051
hub51chicago.com

# Brett Jackson

*may be young, but the Cubs' No. 1 draft pick from 2009 has a head start on eating well. This pasta dish is a favorite of Brett's and his girlfriend, Darby, who has Celiac disease. She can't eat gluten, which is found in most flour and wheat products, including pasta. When baked for around 30 minutes, the spaghetti squash begins to soften, and when scraped out of its pumpkin-like casing it "noodles," Darby said. Spaghetti squash is a light carbohydrate and low calorie vegetable, which makes it a great substitute for pasta for anyone trying to cut back on calories, gluten and/or carbohydrate intake. Brett said the recipe is very flexible from the vegetables used to the meat used. "I like to use ground buffalo meat in the sauce because I like how lean the meat is and think it's pretty tasty," Brett said. "But you can be creative with your protein base." Eat on.*

## Buffalo Spaghetti Squash Pasta

Serves 2

### Ingredients

- 1 spaghetti squash, halved lengthwise and seeded
- 1 lb. ground buffalo meat
- 2 Tbsp. vegetable oil
- 1 onion, chopped
- 1 zucchini chopped
- 1 clove garlic, minced
- 1 1/2 cups chopped tomatoes
- 3/4 cup crumbled feta cheese
- 3 Tbsp. sliced black olives
- 2 Tbsp. chopped fresh basil

### Directions

**1.** Preheat oven to 350 degrees.

**2.** Lightly grease a baking sheet. Place spaghetti squash cut sides down on the prepared baking sheet, and bake 30 minutes in the preheated oven, or until a sharp knife can be inserted with only a little resistance.

**3.** Remove squash from oven, and set aside to cool enough to be easily handled.

**4.** Meanwhile, heat oil in a skillet over medium heat. Sauté onion in oil until tender. Add garlic, and sauté for another 2–3 minutes.

**5.** Stir in the tomatoes and zucchini, and cook only until they are warm.

**6.** Pan-fry 1 lb. of ground buffalo meat.

**7.** Use a large spoon to scoop the stringy pulp from the squash, and place in a medium bowl. Toss with the ground buffalo, sautéed vegetables, feta cheese, olives, and basil. Serve warm.

**Ted Lilly** *is the bulldog on the Cubs pitching staff. But when it comes to cooking, he's pretty simple. He called this recipe a "great breakfast dish because it's tasty, easy, and quick." It's all that and a tradition in the Lilly household. "My father taught me how to prepare this dish when I was about 10 years old," Lilly said. You can bet he'll be teaching son, Theo—Theodore Roosevelt Lilly IV—who was born in March 2010, the same concoction in a few years. "I don't cook much at all," Ted said, "but every once in a while, I'll make this if we have friends or family over." Sometimes simple is good.*

## Egg In The Hole

Serves 1

### Ingredients

1   slice whole wheat bread
1   egg
    butter

### Directions

**1.** Take a slice of whole wheat bread and puncture a hole about 1$\frac{1}{2}$ inches in diameter in the center. You can use a glass to carve out the hole. Save the cut bread circle.

**2.** Lightly butter the bread and put it on a frying pan at medium low heat. Crack the egg, drop it inside the hole in the bread, and cook for about 1 minute. Flip and cook to desired doneness.

**3.** Use the circle as a dipper for the egg yolk.

# *Fergie Jenkins'* wife, Lydia, shared

*this recipe, which is a favorite dish of theirs. She also shared the story behind the recipe: "Fergie has always been an avid hunter, even during his playing days. I was never introduced to any kind of wild game before we met. However, he had gotten all these pheasants during a hunt, so I finally decided to try cooking them in a manner that I thought would make them taste tolerable. Fergie gave me this recipe and lo and behold it turned out great, and I loved it! (It tastes just like chicken.) I still can't quite go for the deer meat. Oh well, maybe he'll come up with another recipe."*

## Fergie's Bagged Pheasant

Serves 4–6

### Ingredients

1 chicken bouillon cube, dissolved in ½ cup hot water

1 envelope dry onion soup mix

1 orange, peeled and cut into pieces

½ cup white wine

½ cup water

salt to taste

pepper

3–4 pound pheasant, cut into pieces (can also substitute chicken for pheasant)

### Directions

1. Preheat oven to 250 degress.

2. Combine all ingredients except pheasant in a bowl; mix well.

3. Place pheasant in a cooking bag; pour in seasoning mixture.

4. Seal bag and slow roast for 4–6 hours.

# WILDFIRE®
## STEAKS, CHOPS & SEAFOOD

## *Derrek Lee* is a creature of habit.

*Whenever the Cubs first baseman goes to Wildfire restaurant in Chicago, he orders the same thing: the Parmesan crusted filet. Derrek, his wife, Christina, daughter, Jada, and son, Dylan, do go out but most often spend evenings at home. Christina is the top chef in the family. "She cooks pretty much anything—fish, spaghetti, fried chicken, meatloaf," Derrek said. She's even learned an oyster dressing from his grandmother that is a perfect complement to turkey. In the off-season, the Lees go to his grandmother's house for Sunday meals. "My grandmother mixes it up—she's a really good cook," he said. Jada has an unusual favorite request: She likes sushi. Derrek also has a routine at Wrigley Field. "In Chicago, I eat scrambled eggs with ham and cheese every morning," he said. Does home clubhouse manager Tom "Otis" Hellman know that? "Yes," Derrek said. "I've done it every day since I've been in Chicago." Wildfire chef Joe Decker created this recipe. Note that you need to make the Parmesan topping the day before.*

## Wildfire Parmesan-Crusted Filet

Serves 8

### Ingredients

**Topping Ingredients**

- 1/2 lb. softened, unsalted butter
- 1 cup finely grated Parmesan cheese (Grana Parmesan preferred)
- 1 cup panko bread crumbs
- 1 tsp. finely minced garlic
- 2 Tbsp. finely minced shallots
- 1/2 tsp. kosher salt
- 1/4 tsp. fresh ground black pepper
- 1 tsp. chopped fresh thyme
- 1/4 cup finely chopped parsley

**Filet Ingredients**

- 8 pieces of 8 oz. center-cut beef tenderloin steaks
- 4 Tbsp. melted, unsalted butter
- 1 Tbsp. of kosher salt
- 1 tsp. of cracked black pepper

### Directions for Topping

**1.** Whip butter in a stainless steel bowl with electric mixer until light and fluffy (2–3 minutes). Scrape down the bowl with a spatula and mix the remaining ingredients well.

**2.** Place a rectangular piece of plastic wrap on a work table. Scrape the softened topping mix evenly in the middle of the sheet of plastic wrap. Roll into a log shape and wrap well. Refrigerate overnight.

**3.** When ready to serve, slice 1/2-inch-thick discs and keep ready to top on each filet.

### Directions for Filet

**1.** Take steaks out of refrigerator and leave at room temperature for 30 minutes.

**2.** Brush steaks well with melted butter. Season steaks evenly with kosher salt and cracked black pepper.

**3.** Place on grill or in broiler and cook until just desired temperature. Top with sliced Parmesan crust and finish on grill or in broiler until golden brown.

Wildfire
159 W. Erie St., Chicago, IL
(312) 787-9000
wildfirerestaurant.com

One of *Ted Lilly*'s perks of playing day games in Chicago is the opportunity to eat at the city's variety of restaurants for dinner. The Cubs pitcher takes full advantage of that. One of the lefty's favorite places is Stanley's Restaurant in Lincoln Park, which provided this recipe. Serve it with tortilla chips and cold beer.

## Stanley's King of Chilis

Serves 8–10

### Ingredients

- ½ lb. butter
- 3 onions, finely chopped
- 4 ribs of celery, finely chopped
- 3 green bell peppers, finely chopped
- 4 Tbsp. garlic, chopped
- 1 bay leaf
- 3 lbs. ground beef
- 2 lbs. chorizo
- 4 Tbsp. ancho chili powder
- 3 Tbsp. quajillo chili powder
- 3 Tbsp. smoked Spanish paprika
- 5 Tbsp. ground cumin
- ⅓ can chipotles in adobo, minced
- 3 Tbsp. dried oregano leaves
- 1 Tbsp. ground coriander
- 1 cup tomato paste
- 3 cans or bottles beer, 12 oz. each
- 3 quarts canned tomato filets (or canned tomatoes)
- 5 Tbsp. sugar
- salt and pepper to taste

### Directions

**1.** In a large pot, sweat onions, celery, and peppers in butter over medium heat, until translucent.

**2.** Add garlic and continue to sweat for another 2 minutes.

**3.** Add ground beef and chorizo; continue to cook until beef and chorizo are cooked through.

**4.** Add spices and tomato paste; mix well with meat mixture and cook for 5 minutes.

**5.** Add beer, reduce liquid by half.

**6.** Add tomatoes, sugar, salt, and pepper.

**7.** Continue cooking on low heat for 20 to 25 minutes; skim off any fat from the top, if necessary.

**8.** Season with salt and pepper.

**9.** Garnish with pico de gallo, sour cream, pickled jalapeños, and tortilla chips.

Stanley's Kitchen and Tap
1970 N. Lincoln Ave., Chicago, IL
(312) 642-0007
stanleyskitchenandtap.com

# Sean Marshall

*likes to grill. Give him a steak, chicken, or salmon, and he's happy. "That's my specialty," Sean said. When the left-handed pitcher was in the Cubs' starting rotation, he could plan his weekly menu. It was usually steaks every fifth night before a start. "My dad cooks good steaks—steak and potatoes," Sean said. "It's a guy thing. It's a masculine meal, steak and potatoes. That's the way to go." He'll expand his food selection for Italian food, too. His girlfriend, Sarah, wowed Sean with this meatloaf recipe, which was handed down from her mother.*

## Sarah's Mom's Masterpiece Meatloaf

Serves 4

### Ingredients

- 1 lb. ground beef (or ground turkey)
- 1 small green pepper, chopped
- 1 medium onion, chopped
- 1 sleeve snack crackers
- 1 Tbsp. minced garlic
- 3/4 cup barbeque sauce
- salt and pepper to taste

**Crust Ingredients**
- 1 sleeve snack crackers
- 1/2 to 3/4 cup barbeque sauce

### Directions

1. Preheat oven to 350 degrees.
2. Mix all meatloaf ingredients in a bowl.
3. Shape into two small loaves.
4. Mix the ingredients for the crust in a bowl.
5. Pat the crust mixture on top of the two loaves.
6. Bake on a broiler pan for 45 minutes to 1 hour.

# *Carmelo Martinez* is a popular guy

*during spring training. The Cubs' Latin American field coordinator is very comfortable in the kitchen and will make traditional Puerto Rican and Dominican meals for the players and coaches. One staple is chicken with rice, or arroz con pollo. His grandmother, Cruz Maria, taught him how to cook. She worked in a school for 30 years and wanted to make sure Carmelo would be all right when he went to the United States to play in the big leagues. At the age of 14, he learned a few meals. "I had to take care of myself," he said. Most of the young Latin players in the Cubs' minor league system also can cook but aren't allowed to do so in hotels. Some use a rice cooker but Martinez prefers to use a pan because he can slightly burn the rice on the bottom of the pan—a treat called "con con" in the Dominican. "Everybody loves that," Martinez said. "It's crunchy. If you cook in a rice cooker, you don't get that." We like this recipe for arroz con pollo and got Carmelo's approval.*

## Chicken with Rice (Locrio de Pollo)

Serves 4

### Ingredients

- 4  lbs. of chicken, cut into pieces
- 4  cups rice
- 7  cups water
- 5  Tbsp. of oil
- 1  tsp. of sugar
- 1/4  cup tomato paste
- 1/4  cup green chilies, diced
- 1  pinch oregano
- 1  tsp. minced garlic
- 1  pinch of black pepper
- 2  tsp. sliced green olives
- 1/4  cup celery, large dice
- 1  Tbsp. minced parsley
- 1  Tbsp. minced cilantro
- 1/2  tsp. thyme
-   salt

### Directions

**1.** Rinse chicken pieces in cold water, pat dry with paper towel, and rub with a bit of lemon.

**2.** Marinate chicken in the chilies, garlic, oregano, pepper, olives, parsley, cilantro, and thyme.

**3.** In a Dutch oven, heat 3 Tbsp. of oil and add the teaspoon of sugar. Let the sugar heat until it caramelizes and turns dark brown, taking care not to burn it. Add the chicken pieces and lightly brown. Cover pan and cook on medium for 10 minutes.

**4.** Add the tomato paste and stir. Season with salt to taste. Add the water and stir, bringing to a boil. Add the rice and continue cooking on medium heat, stirring frequently so that the rice does not stick to the pan's bottom.

**5.** Cook until the water has evaporated. Cover the pan tightly, reduce heat to low, and cook gently for 15 minutes. Check to see that the rice is fully cooked, then rest for 5 to 10 minutes. Stir in remaining oil and check seasonings. Garnish with additional parsley and cilantro. Serve at once.

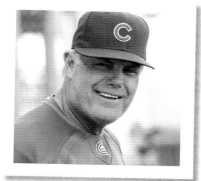

*Lou Piniella* has to be careful about what he eats. The Cubs manager has Type 2 diabetes, so his wife, Anita, monitors his food intake. "We eat a lot of healthy-type meals in the winter, like casseroles and chicken salad and tuna fish," Lou said. Anita does make a terrific paella, which the entire Piniella clan enjoys together. That was one option for this cookbook, but she thought the recipe was a little too complicated. She also considered one with spinach but then confessed that Lou won't eat that. He stays out of the kitchen. "I've never cooked," he said. "My wife will cook paella, lasagna, and I'll get the steaks out. We have the kids and family over every Sunday. When I get involved, it's just with the grill and steaks." Lou also says he can handle omelets pretty well. When they're in Chicago, the Piniellas take advantage of the variety of restaurants. "Eating at home is a takeout meal," he said. "If we're winning, I go out a little more. If not, I tend to stay in." Let's hope he's eating out a lot.

## Anita Piniella's Layered Chicken Salad

Serves 6–8

### Ingredients

- 4 cups shredded iceberg lettuce
- 1/4 lb. bean sprouts
- 8 oz. can water chestnuts, drained and sliced
- 1 medium cucumber, thinly sliced
- 1/2 cup thinly sliced green onions
- 4 cups cooked chicken (2- to 3-inch strips)
- 2 6 oz. packages frozen pea pods, thawed
- 2 cups mayonnaise
- 2 tsp. curry powder
- 1 Tbsp. sugar
- 1/2 tsp. ground ginger
- 1/2 cup Spanish peanuts
- 6 cherry tomato halves

### Directions

**1.** In a shallow 4-quart serving dish, layer the ingredients, beginning with the lettuce, then the bean sprouts, water chestnuts, cucumber, green onions, chicken, and pea pods.

**2.** In a small bowl, combine mayonnaise, curry powder, sugar, and ginger. Spread the mixture on top of the layered ingredients. Cover and refrigerate. This can be chilled as long as 24 hours.

**3.** When ready to serve, sprinkle the peanuts and tomatoes on top.

# Corey Miller

*and his fiancée, Maria Myaskovsky, were having dinner one night at a restaurant and both raved about one of the pasta dishes they ordered. "She said, 'I can make this,'" said Corey, one of the Cubs bullpen catchers. "She said, 'Any meal you like, I can duplicate that.'" That was definitely an attractive offer. Somehow, Maria is able to determine the ingredients simply by taste. So that week, she made this chicken pasta dish. "She duplicated it—but it was even better because it was made with love," Corey said. "We always have this meal. It's our No. 1 meal." So try it and see if your guests can guess the ingredients.*

## Corey & Maria's Chicken Pasta

Serves 2

### Ingredients

- 1 lb. chicken breast
- 16 oz. Alfredo sauce
- 1/4 cup diced sun-dried tomato
- 6 slices cooked bacon
- 1/2 cup frozen peas
- 5 oz. bowtie pasta
- salt (or seasoned salt) and pepper

### Directions

**1.** Cook the bacon and break it into pieces. Set aside.

**2.** Cook the chicken breast. Add salt and pepper to taste. (We prefer seasoned salt.) Shred and set aside.

**3.** Cook bowtie pasta according to package directions. During the last couple minutes of the pasta cooking, add the peas. Drain.

**4.** Over low heat, mix all of the ingredients together and let sit for 5 minutes. Serve.

## Ahi Tuna Tartare, Lime, Chile, Avocado, and Crispy Papadum Chips

Recipe by Michael Shrader, Executive Chef

### Ingredients

- 4 oz. sushi-grade ahi tuna, cut into $1/4$-inch cubes
- $1/2$ ripe avocado, cut into $1/4$-inch cubes
- $1/2$ jalapeno chili, finely chopped (if you don't want heat, then discard seeds before chopping)
- $1/2$ fresh lime
- 2 Tbsp. extra virgin olive oil
- $1/2$ large package papadums (Indian chick pea wafers—cook in microwave until crispy, break into smaller chips)
- sea salt, to taste

### Directions

**1.** Mix all ingredients into bowl (except papadums). Adjust seasoning to taste (salt & lime juice).

**2.** Serve chilled on a cold plate or bowl. Place papadum chips on the side and use to scoop out tuna.

**Note:** Serve all ingredients extremely cold.

N9NE Steakhouse
440 W. Randolph St., Chicago, IL
(312) 575-9900
n9negroup.com

## Grilled Thick French Toast

Serves 6–8

### Ingredients

- 6 large eggs
- 1/2 cup whole milk
- 1 tsp. ground cinnamon
- 1 Tbsp. pure vanilla extract
- 1/2–1 oz. clarified margarine
- 1 2 lb. loaf seedless Greek bread
- 1/2 cup white confectionary sugar

### Directions

**1.** Combine eggs and milk. Add cinnamon.

**2.** Add vanilla extract and mix thoroughly. (Make sure there are no signs of the cinnamon in the mix.)

**3.** Cut Greek bread (or a dense white flour bread) into 1 1/2-inch-thick slices.

**4.** Dip each slice of bread into the batter, turning on each side to thoroughly coat. Let the excess batter drain off. (Bread may be placed on a tray or cookie sheet to hold until cooking.)

**5.** Add clarified margarine (cooking spray may be substituted) to a flat griddle or large frying pan. Heat on medium-high setting.

**6.** Add coated bread slices and cook until golden brown. Flip over and cook other side until golden brown. Remove from griddle. Cut on a diagonal.

**7.** Place French toast on plate and sprinkle a liberal amount of white confectionary sugar over top. You are ready to serve!

Lou Mitchell's
565 W. Jackson Blvd., Chicago, IL
(312) 939-3111
loumitchellsrestaurant.com

*Xavier Nady* doesn't like leftovers but his wife's meatloaf is the exception. It's one of the few things he will eat the next day. The Nadys try to eat healthy. "I go through phases," Xavier said. "I might eat healthy for a couple days. But if we go have Mexican, I'll have four baskets of chips before the food gets there. I have my weaknesses—bread and butter before dinner." What "X" has learned is that as you get older, you have to watch your food intake and take care of yourself a little better to stay in the game. "There are times I'll eat McDonald's," he said. "I just try not to do it on a daily basis. When you're traveling, it's a lot harder and when you have a kid it makes it a little difficult, too." Wife Meredith was worried this recipe would be too boring, but it's tasty. Xavier also loves his mother's cheesecake recipe, which Meredith suggested. But, she cautioned, "It's not as healthy but a favorite." Maybe we'll sneak it in the next cookbook.

## Xavier & Meredith Nady's Meatloaf

Serves 2–4

### Ingredients

- 1/2 lb. lean ground turkey meat
- 1/2 lb. extra lean ground turkey meat
- 1 6 oz. can of tomato paste
- 1 egg
- 6 reduced-fat thin wheat crackers, crushed
- 1 packet dried soup mix, onion mushroom flavor
- splash of milk
- 1 small can tomato sauce

### Directions

1. Preheat oven to 375 degrees.

2. In a large bowl, mix together turkey meat, tomato paste, egg, wheat crackers, soup mix, and a splash of milk. Put mixture into greased loaf pan.

3. Cook in oven for 30 minutes. Pour desired amount of tomato sauce on top of the meatloaf. Continue cooking for another 30 minutes.

*Coach* **Mike Quade** *is a foodie. He's the first to admit it. He seeks out new, inter-esting restaurants on the road and he's not afraid to experiment. But when he gets home, Mike can usually be found on the water, searching for dinner. Here's his fish story. "For nine months a year, it's basically all baseball all the time," he said. "However, once I get home for the winter, my time is consumed by two of my other passions—fishing and cooking. My home along the Florida Gulf Coast affords me with some of the best shallow saltwater fishing in the country, and the only thing better than the challenge of catching these fish is the fun of preparing them." Mike has a variety to choose from: snook, redfish, trout, and flounder. Here, he's submitted one of his favorite ways to prepare snook filets. This will work with any other firm whitefish. The man known as "Q" likes to serve this with roasted potatoes, sweet corn relish, and blue cheese and pear salad. He knows food.*

## Pecan-Crusted Snook with Cajun Cream Sauce

Serves 2

### Ingredients

2  6 oz. snook filets (or other firm whitefish filets)
$1/2$  cup flour
$1/2$  cup pecans, chopped and toasted
$1/2$  cup bread crumbs (panko preferred)
1  egg
1  tsp. Dijon mustard
$3/4$  tsp. any favorite Creole spice
1  shallot, chopped
2  Tbsp. butter

**Sauce**
$1/2$  cup white wine
$1/2$  cup cream
$1/4$  cup Dijon mustard
$1/3$  tsp. Creole spice
  pinch of cayenne pepper
  salt and pepper to taste

### Directions

**1.** Preheat oven to 375 degrees.

**2.** Mix flour and Creole spice in one bowl. Mix pecans, bread crumbs, and shallot in another bowl. Whisk egg and mustard in a third bowl.

**3.** Coat each filet with flour mixture, shaking off excess, then coat with egg mixture, and finally press each filet firmly on both sides into the pecan mixture.

**4.** Melt 2 Tbsp. of butter in a sauté pan or cast-iron skillet over medium heat and sauté both filets for 2–3 minutes on each side.

**5.** Transfer to a cookie sheet and finish baking in the oven for 8–10 minutes depending on filet thickness.

**6.** While fish is baking, deglaze sauté pan with $1/2$-cup wine and let that reduce a few minutes.

**7.** Add cream, mustard, and spices to sauté pan and stir to blend. Simmer for 3 minutes.

**8.** To serve, put a couple tablespoons of sauce on a plate and place a filet on top of sauce.

ITALIAN STEAKHOUSE & BAR

*How does* **Aramis Ramirez** *hit home runs? He waits for a pitch he likes in his zone. What also helps is a few prime steaks in his diet. The Cubs third baseman has a good source—he's a frequent diner at Harry Caray's Restaurant. We've included a recipe here for something else Aramis likes: Harry's crab cakes. Maybe the fresh crab reminds him of the seafood he can get in his native Dominican Republic. Or, maybe they help on those RBI hits.*

## Harry Caray's Jumbo Lump Crab Cakes

Serves 12 (3 oz. servings)

### Ingredients

¼ cup finely diced red onion
¼ cup finely diced red and yellow pepper
2 Tbsp. thinly sliced scallions
¾ cup panko breadcrumbs
½ cup heavy cream
1 Tbsp. Dijon mustard
1 tsp. Worcestershire sauce
1 tsp. hot pepper sauce
1 tsp. Old Bay® seasoning
½ tsp. granulated garlic
1 egg
1 egg yolk
   salt and pepper
2 Tbsp. lemon juice
1½ lbs. jumbo lump blue crab meat
⅓ stick butter
½ cup flour
2 cups remoulade sauce

### Remoulade Ingredients

2 cups mayonnaise
¼ cup chopped capers
¼ cup finely diced red onion
¼ cup Dijon mustard
½ tsp. Old Bay seasoning
½ tsp. paprika
½ tsp. Worcestershire sauce
½ tsp. hot pepper sauce
1 tsp. lemon juice
   salt
   pepper

### Directions

1. Preheat oven to 400 degrees.

2. In a large mixing bowl, combine the red onion, peppers, scallions, breadcrumbs, heavy cream, Dijon mustard, Worcestershire sauce, hot pepper sauce, Old Bay seasoning, garlic, egg, egg yolk, salt and pepper to taste, and lemon juice.

3. Gently fold in the crab meat, being careful not to break up the lumps. Form into 3-ounce patties.

4. In a sauté pan, melt the butter over medium heat. Lightly dust the crab cakes with flour so they don't stick to the pan. Brown the crab cakes on each side, about 1 minute per side. Transfer the cakes to a baking sheet and bake in the oven for 5–7 minutes.

5. Serve with the remoulade sauce.

Remoulade Sauce Directions

1. Combine the mayonnaise, capers, red onion, mustard, Old Bay seasoning, paprika, Worcestershire sauce, hot pepper sauce, lemon juice, and salt and pepper to taste in a medium bowl.

Makes 3 cups

Harry Caray's Chicago
33 W. Kinzie St., Chicago, IL 60610
(773) HOLY-COW
harrycarays.com

# WILDFIRE®
## STEAKS, CHOPS & SEAFOOD

*Larry Rothschild* grew up in Chicago and knows the city well. He has several favorite restaurants he likes to frequent, and Wildfire is at the top of his list. The Cubs pitching coach always orders the same thing—Wildfire's spit-roasted herb chicken. Maybe it's part of his coaching philosophy. Rothschild wants the Cubs pitchers to be consistent, too. This recipe is definitely a winner.

## Wildfire Spit-Roasted Herb Chicken

Serves 2–4

### Ingredients

- 1 Tbsp. minced fresh thyme
- 1 Tbsp. minced fresh sage
- 1 Tbsp. minced fresh rosemary
- 1 Tbsp. minced fresh parsley leaves
- zest and juice of one lemon
- 1 Tbsp. minced garlic
- 2 tsp. kosher salt
- 1/2 tsp. fresh ground black pepper
- 1/4 tsp. crushed red chilies
- 2 Tbsp. extra virgin olive oil
- 2 Tbsp. canola oil
- 1 natural whole chicken (3 1/2 lbs.)

### Directions

**Note:** At Wildfire, we roast the chicken on a wood-burning rotisserie. You may use a rotisserie feature on your home grill. One other method would be to split the chicken in half, remove the backbone, and roast in a 400-degree oven.

1. Mix all ingredients, except chicken, to create a marinade.

2. Rub the chicken well with the marinade—under the skin, in the cavity, and evenly over the entire bird.

3. Marinate the chicken for 24 hours in the refrigerator.

4. Cook chicken using your home grill's rotisserie or in the oven for 40 minutes, or until a meat thermometer registers 165 degrees.

5. Carve as desired.

Wildfire
159 W. Erie St., Chicago, IL
(312) 787-9000
wildfirerestaurant.com

# *Ryne Sandberg*'s wife, Margaret,

knows a quick and simple way to please her kids: her version of chicken tacos. "My kids always ask for them for their birthday dinner," Margaret said. "I have no measurements. I just do it by looks and taste—that's just the way I cook. My girls don't understand when I tell them to add this or that, with no amounts!" The recipe sounds a little like a quesadilla but after cooking, Margaret adds the lettuce, more cheese, salsa, and guacamole, or whatever topping you like. "They are so good," Margaret said. "Maybe not the healthiest but delicious, if I say so myself." Sounds like a Hall of Fame—worthy meal.

## Margaret Sandberg's Chicken Tacos

Serves 4–6

### Ingredients

- 1  cooked roasted chicken, meat shredded
- 2  cups shredded yellow cheese
- 1  can diced green chilies
- ½  cup sour cream
- 1  package corn tortillas
   vegetable oil

**Toppings**
   guacamole
- 2  cups shredded lettuce
   shredded cheese
   salsa

### Directions

**1.** Mix shredded chicken, yellow cheese, chopped green chilies, and sour cream together.

**2.** Place a small amount of mixture into the fresh corn tortillas, fold in half and fry them in a frying pan, in about a half-inch of hot oil. Hold taco with tongs.

**3.** Turn once to cook both sides. Remove and place on paper towels to absorb some of the grease. Open each taco and add shredded lettuce, cheese, salsa, and guacamole.

ITALIAN STEAKHOUSE & BAR

When in Chicago, *Ryne Sandberg* almost always dines at Harry Caray's Italian Steakhouse. It's not just the good food—particularly the rigatoni with vodka sauce featured here—but also the Chicago sports memorabilia that draws fans. The restaurant displays several items from Ryne's playing days with the Cubs, including the bat he used to hit the first home run in the 1989 playoffs at Wrigley Field. It's like a Cubs Hall of Fame, which is fitting for No. 23.

## Harry Caray's Rigatoni with Vodka Sauce

Serves 4

### Ingredients

- 1 lb. rigatoni, cooked al dente
- 1/4 cup olive oil
- 4 Roma tomatoes, diced
- 3 shallots, diced
- 6 cloves fresh garlic, finely chopped
- 1/4 cup chopped fresh basil leaves
- 1/2 cup vodka
- 1 cup Alfredo sauce
- 2 cups marinara sauce
- 1/2 cup mascarpone cheese
- 1/2 cup shaved Parmigiano-Reggiano cheese
- salt
- pepper

### Directions

**1.** Heat a large sauté pan over medium heat. Once the pan is hot, add the olive oil, tomatoes, shallots, garlic, and basil. Sauté until the shallots are translucent and the garlic is lightly browned.

**2.** Remove from heat and deglaze the pan with the vodka. Simmer until reduced by one-quarter and add the alfredo sauce, marinara sauce, and mascarpone cheese. Bring the mixture to a simmer and toss with the rigatoni.

**3.** Add the Parmigiano-Reggiano immediately prior to serving.

**4.** Add salt and pepper to taste.

Harry Caray's Chicago
33 W. Kinzie St., Chicago, IL 60610
(773) HOLY-COW
harrycarays.com

# Carlos Silva

*Carlos Silva was thrilled when he learned that his mother, Zulay, was granted a 10-year visa to the United States. Not only would his biggest fan be able to watch him in person but also his favorite cook would be in town. Arepas are a staple in Venezuela morning, noon, and night. Silva said you can be in his homeland at 5 A.M. and find fresh baked arepas on nearly every street at areperias. The key is the stuffing. Silva's favorite is arepa de pabellon, which is a combination of shredded seasoned meat, black beans, cheese, and plantains. His mother also is known for her empanadas. "When my mother was young, she and my grandmother had a store and they would make them," Carlos said. "The store was very popular." Here's a little taste of Venezuela.*

## Arepas

Makes 5–10 arepas

### Ingredients

- 2 cups pre-cooked cornmeal
- $1/2$ tsp. salt
- 3 cups boiling water
- 3 Tbsp. oil

### Fillings

To fill the arepas, split them in half when finished and scoop out a little of the soft dough filling. Stuff with your chosen filling. Traditional fillings include:

- Arepa de Pabellon: shredded, seasoned meat and black beans.
- Reina Pepeada: chopped chicken, avocado, and mayonnaise mashed together.
- Arepa de Dominó: black beans and crumbled white cheese.
- Arepa de Perico: scrambled eggs with tomatoes, peppers, and onions.

### Directions

1. Preheat oven to 400 degrees.

2. In a large bowl, mix together the cornmeal and salt. Pour in $2^1/2$ cups of the boiling water and mix with a wooden spoon to form a mass. Cover with a towel or plastic wrap and set aside to rest for 5–10 minutes.

3. Using wetted hands, form balls of dough out of about $1/4$ cup of dough and press to form a cake about 3 inches wide and $3/4$ inch thick. If the dough cracks at the edges, mix in a little more water and then form the cakes.

4. Heat the oil in a sauté pan or skillet over medium-high heat. Sauté the patties, a few at a time, to form a light brown crust on one side, 5–6 minutes. Flip and brown on the other side.

5. When all the patties have been browned, transfer them to a baking sheet and bake in the oven for 15 to 20 minutes, or until they sound lightly hollow when tapped. Serve immediately.

*Ryan Theriot* doesn't stray far from his Louisiana roots when he's cooking. Jambalaya is a favorite, and Theriot likes to use Chef John Folse's recipe, provided here. Chef John, who has the restaurants White Oak Plantation and Lafitte's Landing at Bittersweet Plantation, has cooked at Ryan's home. He's also contributing to a fundraising event the Cubs shortstop is planning. "He's just a really good dude," Theriot said. "I love his food. He's obviously good at what he does and he's also willing to help." Folse didn't hesitate when asked for permission to use his jambalaya recipe. When contacted, he was "frog giggin'" somewhere in Louisiana with Chicago chef Rick Trumanto.

## Chef John Folse's Chicken and Sausage Jambalaya

Serves 6–8

### Ingredients

- 3 lbs. cubed chicken
- 2 lbs. sliced smoked sausage
- 1/4 cup shortening or bacon drippings
- 2 cups chopped onions
- 2 cups chopped celery
- 1 cup chopped bell pepper
- 1/2 cup diced garlic
- 8 cups beef or chicken stock
- 2 cups sliced mushrooms
- 1 cup sliced green onions
- 1/2 cup chopped parsley
-   Salt and cayenne pepper
-   Louisiana pepper sauce
- 5 cups long grain rice, uncooked

### Directions

**1.** In a seven-quart, cast-iron Dutch oven, heat shortening or bacon drippings over medium-high heat.

**2.** Sauté cubed chicken until dark brown on all sides and some pieces are sticking to the bottom of the pot, approximately 30 minutes. This is very important as the brown color of jambalaya is derived from the color of the meat.

**3.** Add smoked sausage and stir-fry an additional 10 to 15 minutes. Tilt the pot to one side and ladle out all oil, except for one large cooking spoon.

**4.** Add onions, celery, bell pepper, and garlic. Continue cooking until all vegetables are well caramelized; however, be very careful as vegetables will tend to scorch because the pot is so hot.

**5.** Add stock, bring to a rolling boil, and reduce heat to simmer. Cook all ingredients in stock approximately 15 minutes for flavors to develop.

**6.** Add mushrooms, green onions, and parsley.

**7.** Season to taste using salt, pepper, and pepper sauce. Chef John suggests you slightly over-season because the rice tends to require a little extra seasoning.

**8.** Add rice, reduce heat to very low, cover and cook 30–45 minutes, stirring at 15-minute intervals.

**9.** Do not uncover except to stir.

# For *Alfonso Soriano* and *Carlos Marmol* there's a

small storefront restaurant on North Avenue near Humboldt Park in Chicago that is a little slice of heaven. It's at "Tropical Taste" that Sobeida Minaya cooks some delicacies from the three Cubs' island home, the Dominican Republic. The players often have the restaurant deliver a meal to Wrigley Field

or their Chicago homes when they get a craving for stewed chicken and mangu. "She has everything we like there," Marmol said. "It's small but nice." Mangu is eaten for breakfast, lunch, and dinner, and the only change is what you have on the side. For breakfast, add scrambled eggs and a thick slice of fried salami. Lunch and dinner, it's best with stewed chicken because the mangu can easily handle the sauce. The key is mashing the cooked plantains. The consistency Sobeida strives for is similar to chunky, mashed potatoes. On the road, the players can find Dominican food in New York, but it's impossible in Milwaukee or Pittsburgh. In Chicago, Sobeida takes care of the home cooking.

## Mangu

Serves 6–8

### Ingredients

- 4 unripe green plantains
- 4 Tbsp. butter
- 2 Tbsp. oil
- 2 large red onions, sliced
- 1 Tbsp. vinegar
- 1 cup cold water
- salt

### Directions

**1.** Boil the plantains, adding 2 tsp. of salt to the water. When the plantains are very tender, after about one hour, turn off the heat.

**2.** While the plantains are boiling, heat a tablespoon of oil in a shallow pan. Sauté the onion slices until translucent. Add some salt and the vinegar. Reserve for serving.

**3.** Take the plantains out of the water and mash them with a fork or potato masher to desired consistency. Add the butter and the cold water and keep mashing until smooth.

**4.** Garnish with the onion slices.

After the 2009 season, Lou Piniella called *Geovany Soto* into his office and told the young catcher he needed to get in shape. Soto won the National League Rookie of the Year award in 2008, but struggled to match those numbers in '09. When Soto returned home in the off-season, he hired a personal trainer, went on a steady diet of chicken breasts and tuna, and lost 40 pounds. It was tough because his wife, Luzem, is a terrific cook. Geo's teammates didn't recognize him when he reported for spring training. Arroz con gandules was not on Soto's off-season menu but it is a favorite and a traditional Puerto Rican dish. And best of all, he can eat it during the season. "I'll eat it two, three times a week when I'm playing," he said. Arroz con gandules is usually served with a pork roast, mashed potatoes, or a macaroni salad. "It's usually our main dish for Christmas in Puerto Rico," Geovany said. "Every house, on the 24th of December, you have that. Every house, on New Year's Eve, you have that. If you don't have that in Puerto Rico, I don't know what you're doing." So celebrate Puerto Rican—style.

## Arroz con Gandules

Serves 4

### Ingredients

- 1 cup rice
- 1/2 cup sofrito (see recipe below)
- 1 packet sazon (Spanish/ Mexican seasoned salt)
- 1 tsp. salt
- 1 can gandules (pigeon peas)
- 1 Tbsp. oil
- 2 cups water

### Directions

**1.** In a saucepan, combine the oil, sofrito, sazon, salt, gandules, and water.

**2.** Bring to a boil and add the rice.

**3.** Cook for 30 minutes or by directions on rice package.

## Sofrito

Makes about 2 cups

### Ingredients

- 1 cup yellow onion, minced
- 1/2 cup celery, minced
- 1/2 cup carrot, minced
- 1/2 cup olive oil

### Directions

Reserve and use for soup bases or other sauces. Will keep up to a week in the refrigerator, or it can be frozen.

**1.** Heat a pan over medium heat and add vegetables and oil.

**2.** Cook gently until vegetables are soft and the color of straw, about 30 minutes.

ITALIAN STEAKHOUSE & BAR

Out-of-town sportswriters jump at a chance to cover the Cubs because it means day games, which means they have a night free in Chicago. A trip isn't complete without a stop at Harry Caray's Italian Steakhouse in Chicago. Nearly all order the bone-in Chicken Vesuvio. And it's not just a favorite for the scribes. Cubs catcher Geovany Soto loves the dish. "When I came to the Chicago Cubs as a rookie in 2008, Harry Caray's quickly became my favorite post-game destination," Geo said. "The people at Harry's have treated me like family." Can't get downtown? Try this recipe and you'll feel like inviting Geo over—and maybe even a sportswriter or two.

## Harry's Bone-in Chicken Vesuvio

Serves 4

### Ingredients

- 2   4-lb. whole roasting chickens, cleaned
- 1   cup frozen peas
- 4   large Idaho russet potatoes
- 1/2   cup olive oil
- 10   whole cloves garlic
- 1   tsp. salt
- 1   tsp. pepper
- 1   Tbsp. oregano
- 1   Tbsp. granulated garlic
- 1/3   cup chopped parsley
- 1 1/2   cups white wine
- 1 1/2   cups homemade chicken stock or equivalent amount canned, low-sodium chicken broth

### Directions

1. Preheat oven to 375 degrees.

2. Blanch the peas by placing them in boiling water for one minute, then rinsing with cold water to stop the cooking.

3. Cut each chicken into eight pieces.

4. Peel the potatoes and cut them into quarters length-wise. In a large roasting pan, heat the olive oil over medium heat. Add the potatoes and garlic cloves and sauté the potatoes until golden brown.

5. Deglaze the pan with the white wine and reduce by half. Return the potatoes to the pan. Season potatoes and chicken with the salt, pepper, oregano, granulated garlic, and parsley. Add the chicken stock and transfer the roasting pan to the oven for 45 minutes or until the chicken reaches an internal temperature of 165 degrees.

6. Place the chicken on a serving plate and arrange the potatoes around the chicken. Pour the sauce from the pan over the chicken and sprinkle the peas on top.

Harry Caray's Chicago
33 W. Kinzie St., Chicago, IL 60610
(773) HOLY-COW
harrycarays.com

Infielder *Chad Tracy* *not only likes to hit, he loves to grill. Baseball players are always looking for an edge. Hitters try to figure out what a pitcher is going to throw, and pitchers are trying to outsmart the batter. While tailgating at a Carolina Panthers' NFL game, he saw fans spritzing their chicken with something in a spray bottle. What the heck was that? A secret sauce? Nope, just a little apple cider vinegar that, when sprayed lightly on the meat, keeps it moist. He's used this technique a lot. The Tracys have a huge grill at their Arizona home that is fired up year-round. This is not a marinade but something to spray on the chicken while it's cooking. Don't believe it works? "Try it," Chad said. "Add a little coleslaw, baked beans, and you're good."*

## Vinegar Grilled Chicken

Serves 4

### Ingredients

4   chicken breasts (skin on)
    sea salt
    fresh cracked pepper
    spray bottle full of apple
    cider vinegar

### Directions

**1.** Wash chicken breasts and pat dry. Season liberally with salt and pepper.

**2.** Place on a medium hot grill, skin side down. Spray with vinegar a couple of times.

**3.** After 5 minutes, turn chicken and spray skin side.

**4.** After another 5 minutes, turn chicken again and spray bottom side.

**5.** Continue until chicken is fully cooked (internal temperature of 170 degrees recommended).

# Steve Trout
*pitched for the Cubs from 1983–87 and won 13 games in 1984 when the team won the Eastern Division. No other recipe would be fitting for former Cubs pitcher Steve Trout than one for sautéed rainbow trout. The left-hander, whose nickname, appropriately enough, is Rainbow, said he came up with this concoction while fishing. "I did this in Montana," Trout said. "Get a hook, put a worm on it, and send it out in the stream. When the trout bites the worm, pull in the line—easy as that." This recipe is fairly simple, too. You might want to add a spritz of lemon when serving. As Steve says, "Now you can say you ate a trout by a Trout's recipe."*

## Pan-Fried Trout

Serves 4

### Ingredients

- 4 whole trout
- 2 Tbsp. garlic powder
- 2 Tbsp. onion powder
- 2 tsp. black pepper
- 2 tsp. seafood seasoning
- 1 cup flour
- 1 egg
- 1/4 cup milk
- 1–2 cups panko bread crumbs
- 3 Tbsp. peanut oil or canola oil
- 1/4 cup dry white wine
- 2 Tbsp. butter, unsalted
- 1/4 cup capers drained

### Directions

1. Rinse the trout inside and out and pat dry.

2. In a small bowl, mix garlic powder, onion powder, black pepper, and seafood seasoning.

3. Rub seasoning mix all over the trout. Make sure you get plenty of spice on the inside as well.

4. Using three separate shallow pans, fill one with the flour, one with the milk and egg whisked together, and the last with the panko bread crumbs. Coat the trout in flour, dip in egg wash (completely coating the trout), then roll in panko bread crumbs. Place on a plate.

5. Add oil to a sauté pan and heat on medium-high heat. The pan is hot enough for cooking when a small amount of flour sizzles and scatters.

6. Cook trout on each side for 3–4 minutes. Press the tail down because it may tend to curl up. Turn and cook on the other side for about 3 minutes.

7. Remove trout from pan and set aside on a plate while making the sauce.

8. Drain oil from pan. Before returning to heat, add white wine (pour from a measuring cup not bottle). Return the pan to the heat. (Caution: The wine may flame up, but that's okay. Just wait until the alcohol burns off before proceeding.) Add butter and capers. Cook for a couple minutes and pour over the trout.

For Hall of Famer **Billy Williams**, the 2010 season will be a special one. The Cubs will erect a statue at Wrigley Field to honor the sweet-swinging outfielder. "It's one of the greatest tributes to a player," Billy said. He batted .296 with the Cubs from 1959–74 and was inducted into Cooperstown in 1987. He still helps the team, serving as a special advisor. In spring training, he'll take the time to talk to players, young and old, and offer them his advice. He also knows how to eat. Billy didn't hesitate when asked for his favorite recipe. "My wife's pork chops," he said. Shirley came through with a Hall of Fame recipe.

## Sweet-Swingin' Billy's Grilled Pork Chops

Serves 6

### Ingredients

6   center-cut, bone-in pork chops, 2–3 inches thick

2   bottles Lawry's Steak & Chop Marinade

    seasoned salt

    pepper

    Worcestershire sauce

### Directions

**1.** Cut excess fat from the edges of the pork chops, rinse chops under water, and dry chops with a paper towel.

**2.** Place pork chops in large plastic zip-lock bag, pour in marinade, and shake plastic bag to coat chops. Refrigerate for 30 minutes.

**3.** Preheat grill to medium heat.

**4.** Remove pork chops from plastic bag and place in baking pan. Discard marinade.

**5.** Sprinkle both sides of pork chops with seasoned salt, pepper, and Worcestershire sauce.

**6.** Spray both sides of each pork chop with nonstick cooking spray.

**7.** Grill pork chops for 10–15 minutes on each side or until done.

# *Carlos Zambrano*'s wife, Ismary,

is an excellent cook and can whip up Venezuelan dishes that are the envy of friends. There's just one problem. Venezuelans love cheese and butter. "I always tell [Carlos], the cheese and butter will kill you," said Frank Alvarez, Big Z's personal trainer. Ismary is now using more olive oil. The Cubs' Latin players discovered Moises Mendez's My Arepa restaurant in Mesa, Arizona, and he supplied this recipe. You can get a perro caliente (hot dog) at Mo's place or try this delicious carne desmechada. We've provided the English and Spanish translation for the ingredients.

## My Arepa Carne Desmechada (Shredded Beef)

Serves 6–8

### Ingredients

- 4 lbs. shredded beef, brisket or skirt (de carne para desmechar)
- 1 onion (cebolla)
- 2 red peppers (pimentones rojos)
- 5 mini sweet peppers (ajices dulces)
- 6 garlic cloves (dientes de ajos)
- 2 oz. Knorr beef-flavor base (de sazonador de carne)
- 2 oz. Worcestershire sauce (de salsa inglesa)
- 2 cups beef broth (del jugo de la carne) reserved cooking liquid

### Directions

**1.** Parboil the meat for one hour, then shred. Reserve 2 cups beef broth to be used in the sauce.

**2.** For the sauce, cut the onions, peppers, and garlic into small pieces. In a small amount of oil in a preheated skillet, sauté the onions and garlic until softened.

**3.** Add the peppers, mini sweet peppers, beef base, and Worcestershire sauce to the skillet

**4.** Stir until you reach a boil, and add the beef broth. Stir again, cover, lower to medium heat for 10 minutes, and finally add the beef. Stir and let it cook about 10 minutes.

EXTRA INNINGS

Desserts

Ballplayers are like most people—they like sweets. But the Cubs are trying to avoid an overload of fattening items, so nutritionist Dawn Jackson Blatner came up with this recipe to satisfy both a player's sweet tooth and give him something healthy to munch on. Tom "Otis" Hellman, the Cubs clubhouse manager and chief cook, says these truffles have quickly become favorites. Just don't tell the guys they're good for them.

## Cubs Clubhouse: Peanut Butter Protein Truffles

Serves 8

### Ingredients

- ¹/₂ cup natural peanut butter (natural organic easy spread)
- ¹/₄ cup honey
- 2 Tbsp. vanilla whey protein powder
- ¹/₂ cup rolled oats

### Directions

1. Mix all ingredients together.

2. Form one-inch balls and refrigerate for one hour.

# Sam Fuld

*admits he has a sweet tooth. "A little bit," the outfielder says. "When I was a kid, carrot cake was my birthday cake of choice." He told his wife, Sarah, about his preference and she found a recipe in* Bon Appetit *magazine that she tweaked a little. She also found a way to lower the calorie count by substituting sucralose, a no calorie sugar alternative, and applesauce. See the ingredient options. Using cream cheese for the frosting was not in the original recipe— that was Sarah's idea. One other note from Sarah: "I like to add A LOT of cinnamon." So, go crazy.*

## Carrot Cake with Cream Cheese Frosting

Serves 10

### Ingredients

- 2 cups sugar (or 1 cup sugar and $^1/_2$ cup sucralose sugar alternative)
- $1^1/_2$ cups vegetable oil (or 1 cup applesauce and $^1/_2$ cup vegetable oil)
- 4 large eggs
- 2 cups all-purpose flour
- 2 tsp. baking soda
- 2 tsp. baking powder
- 1 tsp. salt
- 1 tsp. ground cinnamon (or more)
- $^3/_4$ tsp. ground nutmeg
- 3 cups finely grated peeled carrots (about 1 lb.)
- $^1/_2$ cup chopped pecans (or walnuts)
- $^1/_2$ cup raisins

### Frosting

- 4 cups powdered sugar
- 2 8 oz. packages cream cheese, softened to room temperature (or use low-fat cream cheese)
- $^1/_2$ cup (1 stick) unsalted butter, room temperature
- 4 tsp. vanilla extract

### Cake Directions

**1.** Preheat oven to 325 degrees F.

**2.** Lightly grease three 9-inch diameter round cake pans with $1^1/_2$-inch sides. Line the bottoms with wax paper or parchment paper. Lightly grease the waxed paper.

**3.** Using a mixer, beat the sugar and oil (or applesauce and oil) until combined. Add the eggs, one at a time, beating well with each addition. Sift the flour, baking soda, baking powder, salt, cinnamon, and nutmeg into the oil, sugar, and egg mix. Stir in the carrots, chopped pecans, and raisins.

**4.** Pour the batter into the prepared pans, dividing equally. Bake about 45 minutes or until a toothpick inserted into the center comes out clean and the cake begins to pull away from the sides of the pan. Cool the pans on racks, about 15 minutes. Turn out the cakes onto the racks and cool completely.

### Frosting Directions

Using a mixer, beat all ingredients in a medium bowl until smooth and creamy.

### Assembly

Place one cake layer on a platter. Spread the top with one-third of the frosting. Top with another layer of cake and spread that with one-third of the frosting. Top with a final cake layer and spread with the remaining frosting. Cover with a cake dome and refrigerate.

# Tom Gorzelanny *is obsessed with Oreo cookies. "I love them," the Cubs lefty said. He's such a freak for the chocolate wafers with the creamy filling that he researched where they were made—Richmond, Virginia, if you're interested—and wanted teammate Sean Marshall to stop by the plant and pick some up for him. Give Grandma Ruby credit for this recipe. "I found out when I first met [wife Lindsey's] family that her grandmother makes these cookies and my obsession with Oreos makes it pretty easy for me to like these things," Tom said. "Once I had the ones her grandmother made, I made sure [Lindsey] knew how to make them. Every Christmas, we make them. That was their tradition. This past Christmas, I think I ate them all." As for dunking Oreos, Gorzelanny dips the whole cookie into milk. No separating beforehand. And he doesn't mess around with anything but Double Stuff Oreos. The Gorzelannys attended a cooking school together but Tom admits he leaves meal-making to Lindsey. "I don't know if I have the patience to cook," he said.*

## Grandma Ruby's Oreo® Cookie Balls

Yields 25–35

### Ingredients

- 1 package of regular-sized Oreo cookies, crushed
- 1 8 oz. package cream cheese, softened
- 1 package white almond bark

### Directions

**1.** Mix the Oreo cookies and cream cheese together. Roll into walnut-sized balls.

**2.** Refrigerate for at least one hour (can be refrigerated up to 24 hours).

**3.** Melt the almond bark.

**4.** Stick a toothpick in an Oreo cookie ball and dip in almond bark.

**5.** Allow to harden on wax paper.

When *Jim Hendry* was an area scout with the Florida Marlins, he worked for current Cubs special assistant Gary Hughes. Hendry had personally looked at six players who were being considered in the first-year player draft in June. But Hendry was told to wait outside the draft room while the Marlins made their picks.

"I was the typical scout who wanted my guy picked in every round," Hendry said. "Gary had already given me the lecture—'You come in, you learn, you don't talk.'"

When the 11<sup>th</sup> round began, about five of Hendry's players were still available. Hughes then called for Hendry. The young scout, who is now the general manager for the Cubs, thought the Marlins brass wanted his advice. Instead, Hughes told Hendry they had run out of fat-free fig cookies. Would he dash over to the grocery store to pick up some more?

This recipe has nothing to do with the cookies but everything to do with figs. Hendry's friend, Vickie Courville, could get fresh ones from her grandfather's huge fig tree, which was in his backyard in Lafayette, Louisiana. Vickie's mother took clippings from that tree and planted them in her backyard, so she had a fresh supply. Her mother created this recipe.

## Fig Cake

Serves 8

### Ingredients

- 1 cup sugar
- 3 eggs
- 1 cup vegetable oil
- 2 cups flour
- 2 tsp. cinnamon
- 1 tsp. salt
- 1 tsp. baking soda
- 1 cup milk
- 2 cups cooked figs (or 2 cups fig preserves)
- 1 cup pecans

### Directions

**1.** Preheat oven to 350 degrees.

**2.** Cream sugar and eggs together. Add vegetable oil and milk; mix together.

**3.** In a separate bowl, combine the flour, cinnamon, salt, and baking soda.

**4.** Combine the two mixtures in one bowl, adding the pecans and figs. Stir well.

**5.** Pour into a 13" x 9" baking dish.

**6.** Bake for 1 hour. Cool before slicing.

*Here's a Southern treat, courtesy of* **Jim Hendry**'s *significant other, Vickie Courville. when you're watching a Cubs game and need something to munch on. Her grandfather would chop the pecans very fine, using a blender. There is a secret to making this right that ballplayers and fans can appreciate. "It's kind of like a superstitious thing," Vickie said. "You can't let anybody else stir it because it won't turn. You have to continuously stir it for 25 minutes because if you don't, it'll stick to the bottom of the pot and start to burn." And if the Cubs win after you eat these, make some more.*

## Pecan Praline

Yields 12–16 bars

### Ingredients

- 2 cups pecans, finely chopped
- 3 cups sugar
- 1 can evaporated milk
- 1 tsp. vanilla
- 1 stick butter

### Directions

1. Place waxed paper on a cookie sheet.

2. Simmer in a 4-quart pot the sugar, milk, vanilla, and butter over medium heat. Stir continuously for 25 minutes.

3. Stir in chopped pecans.

4. Pour the mixture onto cookie sheet.

5. When praline is cool enough to handle and firm, cut into squares.

# Micah Hoffpauir's grandmother,

*Ernestine, would make a huge batch of these brownies every autumn, on the opening weekend of deer season. Micah and the other hunters would stash them into their gear and try to eat them slowly while sitting in the deer stand. The brownies never last long. Hoffpauir's grandmother passed away in February 2009, and his mother has taken over the tradition. "I guess it's something we'll pass down from generation to generation," Micah said. His wife, Tiffany, tweaked this recipe and added chocolate chips on top. But when she makes the brownies for Micah, she only puts chips on half of the mixture. "I like chocolate chips," Micah said. "I love chocolate chip cookies—I just don't like them on the brownie. I prefer a warm brownie and a nice glass of cold milk and get it on. I can eat a whole pan of them." Every time he smells the brownies baking, Hoffpauir is reminded of his grandma, Ernestine. "She was something else," he said.*

## Grandma Ernestine Adams' Blonde Brownies

Makes 16–20 brownies

### Ingredients

- ¹/₃ cup shortening
- 1 Tbsp. hot water
- 1 cup brown sugar
- 1 egg, slightly beaten
- 1 tsp. vanilla
- 1 cup flour
- ¹/₂ tsp. baking powder
- ¹/₈ tsp. baking soda
- ¹/₂ tsp. salt

### Directions

**1.** Preheat oven to 350 degrees.

**2.** Melt the shortening and water in a small saucepan. Add the sugar and dissolve. Cool to room temperature and add the egg and vanilla.

**3.** In a separate bowl, mix the flour, baking powder, baking soda, and salt.

**4.** Add the shortening/water/brown sugar/egg/vanilla mixture into the flour mixture, a small amount at a time. Stir.

**5.** Spread mixture into a 9" x 9" pan. Sprinkle chocolate chips on top (if desired).

**6.** Bake for 20–25 minutes. The secret is to not cook them too long.

When *Rudy Jaramillo*'s family gathers, one of the favorite treats is cola cake. This is a recipe his wife Shelley learned from her grandmother. Shelley has made this for the Cubs hitting coach for the last 40 years. Rudy likes to top a slice of cake with vanilla ice cream. To do this right, use Mexican vanilla extract. If that's not available, make certain the vanilla you use is vanilla extract, not vanilla flavoring. Shelley also dusts the cake generously with powdered sugar and suggests putting fresh strawberries in the center of the cake or at the base.

## Cola Cake

Serves 15–20

### Ingredients

- 2 sticks butter, softened
- 3 cups sugar
- 5 eggs
- 3 cups flour
- 2 Tbsp. lemon extract
- 3 Tbsp. Mexican vanilla extract
- 6 oz. lemon-lime flavored, non-caffeinated soft drink

### Directions

1. Preheat oven to 325 degrees.

2. Using an electric mixer, cream the butter and sugar together for 20 minutes.

3. Add eggs, one at a time, beating after each addition.

4. Add flour.

5. Add extracts, then gently fold in the lemon-lime soft drink.

6. Pour into a well-greased and floured 12-cup bundt pan.

7. Bake for 1 to 1$\frac{1}{4}$ hours until an inserted toothpick comes out clean.

8. Allow to cool completely and invert on your favorite cake plate.

# Laura Ricketts *submitted this recipe, which comes from her family's maternal grandmother, who most likely learned it from her mother. It's a fairly standard rolled sugar cookie recipe, Laura said. However, there's a slight twist—the addition of almond extract for a little extra flavor. "Traditionally, these were Christmas cookies eaten by our mother and her brothers and sisters with breakfast on Christmas morning," Laura said. "Our family still makes them at Christmas time, but I also make them for all sorts of occasions throughout the year, like Valentine's Day, St. Patrick's Day, Easter, Halloween, etc. I have used this recipe to make softball-shaped cookies for my softball team. You could also decorate them as baseball cookies to enjoy during the season." The entire Ricketts family likes to make these cookies, she said, because everyone can participate. Cut out circles, then add a little white frosting plus some red frosting details for stitching and you have a sweet baseball. This recipe makes approximately two dozen cookies, depending on the size of the cookie cutter.*

## The Ricketts Family Cut-out Vanilla Almond Cookies

Makes approximately 24 cookies

### Ingredients

- $1/2$ cup unsalted butter at room temperature
- $3/4$ cup sugar
- 1 large egg
- $1/2$ tsp. vanilla extract
- 2 cups flour
- $1/4$ tsp. salt
- $1/2$ tsp. baking powder

### Frosting

- 1 tsp. almond extract
- 3 cups powdered sugar
- 2–3 Tbsp. of milk

### Cookie Directions

1. Mix together softened butter, sugar, egg, and vanilla extract.
2. In a separate bowl mix flour, salt, and baking powder.
3. Combine all ingredients together; divide the dough in half.
4. Wrap each half in plastic wrap and place in the refrigerator for at least a couple of hours (preferably overnight).
5. Preheat oven to 375 degrees.
6. Remove one half of the dough from the refrigerator. Lightly flour counter surface and roll out dough to about $1/8$-inch thickness.
7. Use cookie cutters to cut into various shapes and use a thick metal spatula to place the cookies approximately $1/2$-inch apart on a cookie sheet lined with parchment paper.
8. Bake for approximately 8–10 minutes. Check cookies midway though the baking process, and turn the cookie sheet if necessary for even baking.
9. When done, the cookies will appear light golden brown. You do not want them to get dark brown on the bottom or edges.
10. Remove from oven and let cool to room temperature on a cooling rack before decorating.

### Frosting Directions

1. Add almond extract to powdered sugar.
2. Slowly add milk one tablespoon at a time and stir the mixture until it has a somewhat thick but slightly runny texture. Add food coloring if desired.
3. Dip cookies face down into the frosting and let the excess frosting run off. To the wet frosting add colored sugars and whatever other cookie decorations you desire. Set aside until the frosting has completely dried. (This may take a few hours.)
4. After the frosting has dried, Laura suggests using a frosting pen with a much thicker frosting to create additional detailed accents such as red baseball stitching.

For Cubs television broadcaster *Len Kasper* this apple crisp is comfort food. There are some foods that always remind you of home. His mother, Sharon, got the recipe from a friend who had apple trees and gave her some of the fresh fruit. "The first time Len tasted it he said, 'Wow, did you really make that? It's so good I could eat the whole pan,'" Sharon said. Now, whenever apples are plentiful at the farmer's markets in Mt. Pleasant, Michigan, she stocks up. You can make this recipe and freeze it for later. "Whenever Len comes home or we visit him, I bake one," she said. "It freezes well and smells delicious baking on a cold Michigan day." Or try it when you're watching the Cubs play on a cool, October day.

## Apple Crisp

Serves 12

### Ingredients

- 1 cup brown sugar
- 1 cup rolled oats
- 1 cup flour
- 1/2 cup butter, melted
- 3 cups apples, peeled and sliced
- 1/2 cup sugar
- 1 tsp. cinnamon

### Directions

1. Preheat oven to 350 degrees.

2. Mix the brown sugar, oats, flour, and butter in one bowl.

3. Mix the apples, sugar, and cinnamon in another bowl.

4. In a greased 8" x 8" pan, layer half of the oat mixture, top it with all of the apples, then finish with the remaining oat mixture.

5. Bake for 45 minutes.

Pitcher *Jeff Stevens* *can whip up a turkey sandwich that would make Dagwood Bumstead proud. Stevens says he's not much of a cook, but he is a first-rate sandwich maker. He's not shy about what ingredients he uses. "I make pretty big deli sandwiches—I put everything you can imagine on them," the right-hander said. But for this book, he turned to his girlfriend, Christina, for some help. When he was pitching at Triple-A Iowa, she would send him a loaf of this banana bread. It's a big-league quality treat. "It's a little home cooking on the road," Jeff said.*

## Christina's Banana Nut Bread

Makes 1 loaf, serves 6–8

Ingredients

1   cup mashed bananas
    (about two regular
    bananas)
1   cup white flour
$^3/_4$  cup whole wheat flour
2   tsp. baking powder
$^1/_4$  tsp. baking soda
$^1/_2$  tsp. salt
$^2/_3$  cup sugar
$^1/_3$  cup butter, softened
2   eggs
$^1/_2$  cup nuts, chopped
    (walnuts or pecans)

Directions

**1.** Preheat oven to 350 degrees. Grease $8^1/_2$" x $4^1/_2$" x 3" loaf pan.

**2.** Sift together in a large bowl the flours, baking powder, baking soda, salt, and sugar.

**3.** In another large bowl, mix together the butter, eggs, nuts, and mashed bananas.

**4.** Add dry ingredients to the butter and egg mixture. Mix quickly and pour into prepared loaf pan.

**5.** Bake one hour. Cool on a rack, and take loaf out of pan.

**SEAFOOD**
**PRIME STEAK**
**& STONE CRAB™**

# Ryan Theriot *likes to take charge in the kitchen. "I love dessert—I like to bake," the Cubs infielder said. His favorite dish "by far" is bread pudding but he didn't want to submit that recipe because he was afraid the Cubs team nutritionist would scream. There's a lot of sugar in Theriot's bread pudding. How much? "We're talking pounds of sugar," he said, laughing. His second favorite? The Havana Dream Pie at Joe's Stone Crab in Chicago. This recipe is a little complicated—go to Joe's, order it, then try it at home.*

## Joe's Havana Dream Pie

Serves 8–10

### Ingredients

**Tres Leches**

³/₄ cup whipping cream

³/₄ cup sweetened condensed milk

³/₄ cup evaporated milk

**Tres Leches Custard**

2¹/₂ cups Boston custard

2 Tbsp. dulce de leche

**Cake**

1 8-inch white cake

### Tres Leches Directions

**1.** Combine these ingredients and mix well until completely blended.

### Tres Leches Custard Directions

**1.** Warm the dulce de leche. Drizzle over custard in a bowl.

**2.** Fold in dulce de leche. Do not overmix.

### Cake Directions

**1.** Slice white cake in half horizontally. Place halves on parchment paper or on a baking sheet, cut side up.

**2.** Poke holes in both halves. Place bottom half back in pie pan.

**3.** Brush bottom half with 1 cup tres leches.

**4.** Brush cut side of top half with 1 cup tres leches, set aside.

**5.** Spread custard onto cake.

**6.** Place top half of cake on top of custard. Brush top with ¹/₄ cup tres leches.

**7.** Refrigerate at least one hour and up to 24 hours. Serve with whipped cream, dulce de leche, and a sprinkle of cinnamon.

Joe's Seafood, Prime Steak & Stone Crab
60 E. Grand Ave.
Chicago, IL 60611
joes.net/chicago

# Notes

# Notes

# Chicago Cubs Charities

*The Chicago Cubs' community activities and charitable contributions reflect an ongoing partnership between the Cubs and the people of Chicago. These efforts help extend the passion of Cubs fans and the commitment of the Cubs organization to improve the lives of children and families across our city and surrounding areas. With the help of Cubs players and staff, spouses and corporate sponsors, the impact of the Cubs' community activities has created a lasting legacy for the people of this great city.*

Chicago Cubs Charities

### The Cubs' leadership in charitable activity includes:

- More than $15 million donated to organizations serving those in need
- More than 3,000 charitable donation items annually, which help organizations raise an estimated $13 million
- Cubs tickets, offering a seat at beautiful Wrigley Field to fans who might not otherwise have a chance to visit
- Programs introducing thousands of children to baseball each year
- Renovated baseball diamonds for Chicago neighborhoods to continue the city's great passion for America's pastime
- Neighborhood protection activities, helping keep the Lakeview community a strong, vibrant place in which to live, work, and play ball
- Annual fundraising events benefiting our charities and welcoming fans to Wrigley Field
- Participation in meetings, discussions, advocacy groups, charitable organizations, and activities in the neighborhoods around Wrigley Field and throughout the city
- Year-round community service involvement and ongoing relationships with the great people of Chicago

Chicago Cubs Charities is proud to support the Dempster Family Foundation through cash donations, in-kind items, and staff-time donations for Dempster Family Foundation events. Chicago Cubs Charities is delighted to be involved in this cookbook project as it takes great satisfaction in supporting all Cubs players and the work they do for charity.

**Fans can learn more about Cubs community efforts at http://chicago.cubs.mlb.com/chc/community/index.jsp**